Fed Up

30 Hour Famine

TRANSIT

Fed Up

Copyright © 2004 by 30 Hour Famine

Published by W Publishing Group, a Division of Thomas Nelson, Inc., P.O. Box 141000, Nashville, Tennessee 37214.

TRANSIT Senior Editor and Brand Manager: Kate Etue

TRANSIT Editorial Staff: Wendy Wood

Cover Design: KMA Direct Communications

Page Design: Walter Petrie for Book and Graphic Design, Nashville, Tennessee

Library of Congress Cataloging-in-Publication Data

Fed up / by 30 Hour Famine.
    p. cm.
    Summary: A thirty-day devotional guide that explores Bible passages and raises awareness about world wide hunger.
    ISBN 0-8499-4470-8 (softcover)
    1. Christian teenagers—Prayer-books and devotions—English.
2. Hunger—Prayer-books and devotions—English. 3. Bible—Devotional literature. [1. Prayer books and devotions. 2. Hunger.]
I. 30 Hour Famine (Organization)
BV4850.F43 2004
242'.63—dc22   2003022363

Printed and bound in the United States of America

04 05 06 07 08 PHX 5 4 3 2 1

Do You Love By Looks?

The Lord said to Samuel, "Find a man named Jesse who lives there, for I have selected one of his sons to be my new king."

So Samuel did as the Lord instructed him. When he arrived at Bethlehem, Samuel took one look at Eliab and thought, "Surely this is the Lord's anointed!" But the Lord said to Samuel, "Don't judge by his appearance or height, for I have rejected him. The Lord doesn't make decisions the way you do! People judge by outward appearance, but the Lord looks at a person's thoughts and intentions."

Then Jesse told his son Abinadab to step forward and walk in front of Samuel. But Samuel said, "This is not the one the Lord has chosen." Next Jesse summoned Shammah, but Samuel said, "Neither is this the one the Lord has chosen." In the same way all seven of Jesse's sons were presented to Samuel. But Samuel said to Jesse, "The Lord has not chosen any of these." Then Samuel asked, "Are these all the sons you have?"

"There is still the youngest," Jesse replied. "But he's out in the fields watching the sheep."

"Send for him at once," Samuel said. "We will not sit down to eat until he arrives."

From the first 11 verses in 1 Samuel 16

Quick, think of one group at school that you would *never* be seen with—they're too weird, too wild, too boring, too goth, too stoned, too something for your taste. Yet are they excluded from God's command that you love your neighbor as yourself?

Next question: To what extent does their *appearance* put you off? Really, is it the hippy skirts that repel you? Or is it the perfect hair? The Saks labels? Too many tats and piercings, or not enough?

Ah, when will we feel in our gut what our mind tells us is true: that we can't always trust our eyes to give us the whole story about someone?

You get something of an object lesson in the Bible about how Samuel, a judge and prophet in ancient Israel, went about choosing Israel's next king. God had prepped Sam with the mere clue that it would be a son of a certain Jesse in the Jerusalem suburb of Bethlehem. Right off the bat he notices the oldest son, Eliab—tall and handsome. *Hmm, so this must be the next king, huh, God?* Samuel mused silently.

And just as silently, God responded to Samuel, *Don't judge by his appearance or height. . . . The Lord doesn't make decisions the way you do! People judge by outward appearance, but the Lord looks at a person's thoughts and intentions.*

Who are the underdogs at your school, in your world, in your global awareness? As a child of God yourself, what kind of love do you owe them?

Love Means Giving Second Chances— And Third, And Fourth, And Fifth . . .

Love means giving second chances
and third, and Fourth, and Fifth...

> After some time Paul said to Barnabas, "Let's
> return to each city where we previously preached
> the word of the Lord, to see how the new believers
> are getting along." Barnabas agreed and wanted to
> take along John Mark. But Paul disagreed strongly,
> since John Mark had deserted them in Pamphylia
> and had not shared in their work. Their
> disagreement over this was so sharp that they
> separated. Barnabas took John Mark with him and
> sailed for Cyprus. Paul chose Silas, and the
> believers sent them off, entrusting them to the
> Lord's grace.
>
> Acts 15:36–40

John Mark was a loser. A slacker. Unable to handle the tough stuff, he bailed.

It all started the day his cousin Barnabas walked into his house and invited John Mark to come with him and another apostle—a fiery convert, a certain Paul of Tarsus—to take the good news of the resurrected Jesus elsewhere in the world. John Mark agreed, and the three of them set off by

3

ship from the mainland of Syria to the island of Cyprus. John Mark pitched in and did his share—which probably included a lot of gritty gofer jobs, because he was the youngest. So maybe it's understandable that John Mark blew out of this missionary trip after it barely got started.

It was no surprise that, after the two apostles had returned home and were planning yet another trip, Paul was dead set against letting John Mark come with them again. After all, hadn't he deserted them last time? But Barnabas insisted they give his relative another chance. The disagreement proved lethal to the Paul-Barnabas partnership, and they each went their own way—Barnabas took John Mark on a preaching trip, and Paul found a new companion for the next missionary journey (Acts 15:36–40).

As if John Mark didn't feel rotten enough deserting them mid-trip, now he was indirectly responsible for splitting up a dynamite apostolic team.

The rest of the story is only hinted at in the Bible, but it's likely that, sometime and somewhere down the road, Paul reconsidered. So that the next time you see John Mark's name, Paul is all sentimental and grateful for him.

Something happened. Paul could be pretty sharp tongued when he wanted to, but he wasn't beyond repenting, turning around, and doing what he could to make a bad situation right. John Mark's mistake hurt for a while, but not forever. Paul seems to have forgiven him and welcomed him back onto the team.

So take heart—there is no end of chances that God gives you. What he wants is your heart, not your impressive spiritual stats. Remember, he's in the business of forgiving. Likewise, how willing are you to give someone another chance who has let you down repeatedly? How vulnerable are you? *How much do you love them?*

My Tangled Life

An expert in religious law tried to trap him
(Jesus) with this question: "Teacher, which is the
most important commandment in the law of Moses?"

Jesus replied, " 'You must love the Lord your
God with all your heart, all your soul, and all
your mind.' This is the first and greatest
commandment. A second is equally important: 'Love
your neighbor as yourself.' All the other
commandments and all the demands of the prophets
are based on these two commandments."

Matthew 22: 35–40

Let's just say it plainly: Life is complicated. We are surrounded
with voices that tell us otherwise—celebrities, movies,
Websites, and magazines do their darnedest to convince us
that life is actually simple. If only you follow the four steps to
the Pounds-Be-Gone weight-loss program, all would be
well. If only you take care of your own needs first. If only
you take care of *others'* needs first. If only you think posi-
tively. If only you just say no. If only . . . if only . . . if only . . .

But no such luck. You know that if life at home happens to
be smooth and simple at the moment, all it takes is a grumpy
parent or an irritating brother or sister to complicate things.

Or the demands of your classes or clubs conflicting with those of your job. And the list goes on.

At least God doesn't try to convince you that life is simple. Everything in the Bible points to what your common sense and experience tell you—that life is usually difficult.

Yet love can penetrate this gray, confusing, complicated ambiguity. It's seldom logical, but it works nonetheless. At least that's what Jesus told the some religious leaders who tried to put him on the spot with this trick question: "Teacher, which is the most important commandment in the law of Moses?"

As usual, Jesus sidestepped the trap. "Here it is," he said: "You must love the Lord your God with all your heart, all your soul, and all your mind. This is the first and greatest commandment." He paused a beat, because what was coming was what these self-righteous guys *really* needed to hear. "A second is equally important, and that's to love your neighbor as you love yourself. In fact, all the other commandments and all the demands of the prophets are based on these two commandments."

Life isn't simple, but love makes it simpler. Among all the answers you wished you had but don't, know this: Jesus will never fail you or forsake you (Hebrews 13:5). As complicated as things get at home, with your boyfriend or girlfriend, with jobs and school and your future, you have Jesus walking alongside you in the murk. And he's there to stay.

It's Not Like God Requires
A Whole Lot from Us

It's Not Like God Requires
A Whole Lot from Us

Should we bow before God with offerings of
yearling calves? Should we offer him thousands of
rams and tens of thousands of rivers of olive oil?
Would that please the Lord? Should we sacrifice
our firstborn children to pay for the sins of our
souls? Would that make him glad?

No, O people, the LORD has already told you
what is good, and this is what he requires: to do
what is right, to love mercy, and to walk humbly
with your God.

Micah 6:6–8

Look again at what the prophet Micah wrote that God *doesn't*
want.

If we're not demonstrating our love for other people, God
doesn't want our worship. Now there's a lot of talk, teaching, and preaching about having your heart right with God
before any kind of true worship can occur. Okay, but that's
only *half* the truth. The other half is this: Unless your
behavior toward other people is merciful, no amount of
worship you aim at God scores with him. Even following the
righteous example of a patriarch like Abraham, who was

8

willing to butcher his own *son* if God asked him to, doesn't score with God.

So what *does* God want, anyway?

1. Do what is right.

This is the foundation. If individuals and societies don't do what's right, things start crumbling fast—personal accountability, the care of those with less than we have, government—all sorts of things. Whether you're Enron in downtown Houston or Ellen in second period history, God wants you to do right. It doesn't always pay off in some ways . . . in other ways, it *always* pays off. Whether it pays or not, God still says, *Do what is right*.

And if you're not sure what the right thing is, then start here with two things you *know* are right—namely:

2. Love mercy.

Mercy is—well, *mercy*. It's what you don't deserve. It's being let off the hook. It's a presidential pardon to a death row prisoner. It's Oscar Schindler adding Jews to his list of factory employees in order to save them from the Treblinka ovens.

How do you love mercy today? You don't run across many death row inmates in a typical day, or persecuted minorities . . . or do you? Look at it this way for a moment: Who are those among us, maybe at the fringes of the privileged class you're a member of, who have few, if any, options? Who are the inmates, in the sense of having no options, unlike most of us? What does mercy look like toward such persons?

Part of the answer: Since ancient times a big part of

mercy and of loving your neighbor has always been providing for those with less than you, wherever you find them, but starting close to you.

3. Walk humbly with God.

A self-righteous person is way too absorbed with listing all the shortcomings of others to actually extend mercy to them. Especially when the very idea of mercy undermines their own superior status with God—for self-righteousness feeds on "how exactly I've kept God's law, and what a crummy job you've done trying to keep God's law."

Micah recognized the dark but likely result within those who are successful at this doing-right and loving-mercy stuff: *self*-righteousness, or the perception that, "Hey, I'm knocking myself out following God's law and doing pretty well at it—and I can't help but notice that you *aren't*. Here, I have some rules for you that will improve your spiritual standing with God, so that you can perform up to my level."

There is simply no room, Micah wrote, for believing however so sincerely that you are better than other Christians because of how well you obey God. That kind of thinking takes you to the edge of some very, very serious sin.

Do what is right, love mercy, and live humbly. That's it. And God says that somewhere in there lies eternal life.

So Where Do I Start Helping Others?

> One day an expert in religious law stood up to test Jesus by asking him this question: "Teacher, what must I do to receive eternal life?"
>
> Jesus replied, "What does the law of Moses say? How do you read it?"
>
> The man answered, " 'You must love the Lord your God with all your heart, all your soul, all your strength, and all your mind.' And, 'Love your neighbor as yourself.' "
>
> "Right!" Jesus told him. "Do this and you will live!"
>
> The man wanted to justify his actions, so he asked Jesus, "And who is my neighbor?"
>
> Luke 10:25–29

Leave it to lawyers to draw excruciatingly fine distinctions between common words. "Love your neighbor as you love yourself," Jesus told the lawyer who specialized in church law. Sounds straightforward enough, right? But no, not to a lawyer.

"Ah, but what do you mean by *neighbor*?" asked the lawyer. And it was that question that triggered possibly the best known of all of Jesus' stories. Here is how it may have sounded to those first-century listeners:

There was an accident on the freeway, she had heard on the living room TV from the bathroom, where she was staring at herself applying eye shadow. So the marketing director took the back way into the city that morning. She was tooling along in her '02 Camry when *BAM*, three things happened simultaneously: She heard a shrieking metallic sound, her dash lit up like a Christmas tree, and the car lost power. As it coasted to a stop, she steered it off onto the gravel shoulder. She sighed, then reached for her cell phone to cancel her morning appointments and call AAA for some help, a tow, whatever. She hit speed dial then noticed the reception icon on the phone: blank. No reception. *Jeez*, she thought, *this really* is *the back way to town. Back way as in outback, wilderness, uncivilized, a cell-less society.*

So she turned on her flashers, raised her hood, and waited for someone to drive by.

That particular country road didn't get a lot of traffic during morning hours, but three other vehicles were on that road that morning. The first one was a local church pastor on his day off, headed in his pickup for the mill five miles down the road to buy feed for his chickens. He saw the car, obviously in need of help. It was equally obvious to him that the car wasn't from around there—someone from the city, most likely. He slowed enough to get a look, but not slow enough to give the impression he was stopping. A woman sat in the driver's seat with short, colored hair, dangly earrings, and makeup—as he passed she looked at him hopefully, then despairingly as the pickup cruised past the Camry and kept going.

Even Good Reasons for Not Helping Are Lousy Reasons

Even Good Reasons for Not Helping
Are Lousy Reasons

Jesus replied with an illustration: "A Jewish man was traveling on a trip from Jerusalem to Jericho, and he was attacked by bandits. They stripped him of his clothes and money, beat him up, and left him half dead beside the road.

"By chance a Jewish priest came along; but when he saw the man lying there, he crossed to the other side of the road and passed him by. A Temple assistant walked over and looked at him lying there, but he also passed by on the other side."

Luke 10:30–32

City folk, he thought. The pastor glanced in his rearview mirror at the gaping hood of the Camry on the shoulder of the country road. No telling what kind of woman *she* was. He read the newspapers enough to know how loose the city's morals were, what they permitted, how they let their liquor stores stay open *on the Lord's day,* of all things. He could just see the mousse-haired woman now, sitting at a bar, cradling a drink in one hand, a cigarette in the other, her little red Camry parked outside. On a Sunday, when all good people were in the Lord's house . . .

By the time he got to the feed store, he had all but forgotten about her.

Meanwhile, back on the gravel shoulder, it was another ten minutes before she saw a car approaching from the opposite direction. The stranded marketing director had no way of knowing that this driver was a church youth director, on her way to a meeting of the Youth Ministry Prayer Network. This youth worker felt so isolated working in her small country church, she really looked forward to these monthly meetings of other youth workers. She saw the Camry's situation as she approached and—unlike the pastor who preceded her on this road—was sincerely pained by her inability to stop and help. Someone else with time to help this stranded motorist would certainly be by soon . . . she really, really *needed* the encouragement of her meeting. So on she drove.

It was fifteen minutes before the marketing director heard another car. This one slowed and pulled off the road just ahead of her. She didn't recognize an '82 Volvo when she saw one, but she *did* notice the bumper stickers when the vehicle squeaked to a stop on the gravel and the dust settled. THE RIGHT TO LIVE, THE RIGHT TO DIE, THE RIGHT TO CHOOSE . . . HELP A KID, BE A MENTOR . . . METROPOLITAN AIDS COUNCIL. *The MAC, huh?* thought the marketing director. She recognized the organization's name from her firm's client list.

A thirty-something man got out of the ancient Volvo. "Need some help?" he asked as he walked toward the Camry.

"Do I ever!" she replied. "And thanks for stopping." He

was on the thin side, she noticed . . . and then she remembered the METROPOLITAN AIDS COUNCIL bumper
sticker. *You don't suppose* . . . she thought, but his question
interrupted her musings.

"Then a despised Samaritan came along, and when he
saw the man, he felt deep pity. Kneeling beside
him, the Samaritan soothed his wounds with
medicine and bandaged them. Then he put the man on
his own donkey and took him to an inn, where he
took care of him. The next day he handed the
innkeeper two pieces of silver and told him to
take care of the man. 'If his bill runs higher
than that,' he said, 'I'll pay the difference the
next time I am here.'

"Now which of these three would you say was a
neighbor to the man who was attacked by bandits?"
Jesus asked.

The man replied, "The one who showed him mercy."
Then Jesus said, "Yes, now go and do the same."

Luke 10:33–37

"So what's the problem?"

After a couple attempts at turning over the engine (only
more grinding and shrieking) and five minutes under the
hood, he pronounced her engine in need of some serious
repairs. Unlike hers, his cell service worked way out here,
and a tow truck was soon on its way. He also called a local

mechanic who, he said, took only cash from out-of-towners. She wilted: With a debit card in her purse, these days she carried almost no cash.

"No sweat," the man said. "I'll cover you, and you can mail me a check when you get home." He smiled. "I *do* accept checks from out-of-towners." He retrieved a scrap of paper from his pocket, wrote his address on it, and handed it to the woman. "Need a lift anywhere?"

Within thirty minutes the tow truck had arrived and soon she was riding shotgun in the Volvo into town, where he in fact had been heading. They bumped along for a while—the Volvo's springs and shocks were apparently as old as the body—until she finally felt comfortable asking (casually, she hoped), "So what's your connection to the Metropolitan AIDS Council?"

"I'm a MAC volunteer—home visits, some lightweight counseling, fix meals, hold babies—whatever I can do for anyone with AIDS."

"How'd you get involved?"

"It was after I was diagnosed HIV-positive. I got pretty depressed, figured I was gonna die soon and painfully, so why try anymore? Then a friend of mine heard about MAC, and they sent out a guy who worked with me, educated me with some facts that were new to me, got me on meds that can keep my resistance up and AIDS at arm's length. So far, so good." He turned to her and smiled. "Day at a time. Just like you."

"Yeah," she said, turning to watch the roadside fence posts whir by, "just like me."

"Now which of these three," asked Jesus, "was a neighbor to the stranded marketing director—the pastor, the church youth director, or the HIV-positive activist and AIDS volunteer?"

The lawyer who specialized in church law couldn't even bring himself to say *HIV-positive activist and AIDS volunteer*, for he was known in town for speaking and writing against public funding for AIDS relief and research; he had also publicly doubted the morality of those with HIV and AIDS.

"The one who showed mercy," he said, vaguely, because reporters were present.

"Bingo!" Jesus said. "Now let him be your example. Do what he did."

The moral of this parable is, of course, this: Your neighbor is anyone in your path (or along the gravel shoulder of your road) who needs your help. And *in your path* can be literal, as the Vietnamese kid you pass every day in the school corridor between period 6 and 7. Or *in your path* can mean *within your sphere of influence*. And these days, *that* can be global.

- To whom locally can you show mercy? How? What would it look like?
- To whom globally can you show mercy? How? What would *that* look like?

Don't You Dare Just Believe

You Pharisees are so careful to clean the outside
of the cup and the dish, but inside you are still
filthy—full of greed and wickedness! Fools! Didn't
God make the inside as well as the outside? So
give to the needy what you greedily possess, and
you will be clean all over.

Luke 11:39–41

Here it is—what you've been waiting for: a Very, Very Brief
History of Jewish and Christian Belief.

- Abraham heard and obeyed the voice of God: "Leave
  your townhome, get on the interstate, and don't leave it
  till I tell you." Not really specific. (No wonder Muslims,
  Jews, and Christians alike consider Abraham their
  "father of faith.") And after that, Abraham's children
  and grandchildren and great-grandchildren were all
  commanded to obey the "God of Abraham and of our
  fathers." (Some of Abraham's children did better than
  others at obeying this command.)

- When the Law came down the slopes of Mt. Sinai
  cradled in Moses' arms, belief was, as they say, codi-
  fied. God's words were now engraved in stone (if not

19

in black and white . . . that would come later, when ink was applied to parchment). There was no guessing, no wondering if you heard God clearly in your head or your heart. You say you loved Yahweh? Put your sacrificial doves where your mouth is, and prove it—by obeying the letter of the Law. Of course, it was hoped that one observed the feast days and sacrificed their best fruits and livestock and kept their eyes from wandering to their neighbors' wives because, at the bottom of it all, they actually *loved* Yahweh and believed that keeping the Law was in their best interest. But you know how laws are easy to keep even when you don't believe in them. Laws are *especially* easy to keep when you don't believe in them but want to give others the impression that you *do*.

- Jesus upset the apple cart (and the dove cages and the money tables in the temple) when he reminded his country's religious leaders that if they all kept the letter of the Law but not its spirit, they were missing the point—which, it so happened, was exactly and unfortunately the case. Jesus wouldn't let this rest either, but kept hammering these religious leaders at every opportunity for (among other things) not taking care of people in the lower strata of society—the poor, the lepers, the widows, the maimed. Read it for yourself in the verse above, and in Matthew 23:23–24, when Jesus lowered the boom on the religious leaders for nitpicking their way through figuring out exactly what they owed God to the penny, but meanwhile ignoring issues of justice and mercy.

- Today. You. Your world. What minor deeds of faith might you be obsessing about, meanwhile leaving undone the stuff God *really* wants you to do—matters of justice and mercy right in your sphere of influence?

Don't Just Stand There Believing!

> Suppose you see a brother or sister who needs food or clothing, and you say, "Well, good-bye and God bless you; stay warm and eat well"—but then you don't give that person any food or clothing. What good does that do?
>
> James 2:15–16

Imagine if a guest speaker preached at your church on a Sunday morning and said things like this:

> *Your faith is only as good as what you do, starting with taking care of the physical needs of people who have less than you do.*
>
> *If you're stealing, stop it, and instead get a job so you have enough to give to those in need.*
>
> *If you, having more than you need, see someone who doesn't have enough and is actually in need, how can you not have pity on them and share what you have? If you truly have God's love in you, then don't just talk about it—put some feet to it!**

What the ancient prophets (Isaiah, Micah, and the rest) announced to the kings of Israel and Judah was the same thing Jesus tried to beat into the brains of the Pharisees— and what the apostles drove home to the readers of their letters, which is this: *What you do is at least as important as what you believe—and maybe more.*

Yeah, these could be fightin' words to modern Protestants, whose Reformation forebears became sick to death of how their fifteenth- and sixteenth-century Christianity (read, medieval Roman Catholicism) had degenerated into buying salvation from a vending machine, sort of.

Paying money for God's grace? Keeping track of their big offerings on Quicken and their good works on Excel? Didn't *anyone* in Western Europe remember what the Bible said, that salvation was by faith through grace and could not be earned?

So was born the Protestant Reformation, whose motto (if spiritual revolutions had mottos) could be *Sola fide*—by faith alone. In the uproar that followed, however, that *other* truth— also in the Bible—got lost: that your faith was fine and good, but if your faith didn't trigger *deeds* of justice and mercy and aid, then your fine feathered faith wasn't worth squat.

Bottom line: Your faith is only as good as what you do for those with less than you have. If you call yourself a Christian, you feed the hungry wherever you find them. And if you don't feed the hungry, you may want to ask yourself why exactly it is that you call yourself a Christian.

In case you're wondering, these are pretty darn accurate rephrasings of James 2:14–17, Ephesians 4:28, and 1 John 3:17–18, respectively.

What Rahab Was Versus
What She Did

What Rahab Was Versus
What She Did

> We are made right with God by what we do, not by
> faith alone.
>   Rahab the prostitute is another example of
> this. She was made right with God by her actions—
> when she hid those messengers and sent them safely
> away by a different road.
>
> James 2:24–25

God loved Rahab for the flimsiest of reasons. Go ahead—read the details in the Old Testament (Joshua, chapters 2 and 6).

She was a pagan, not a Jew. She worshiped idols, not Jehovah. She was a streetwalker, not a saint. She went through men like they were paper towels. These points against her notwithstanding, when General Joshua dispatched a pair of spies to Jericho to do some pre-invasion recon, whose house did they end up in?

You guessed it.

So when the police got a tip about a couple of suspicious strangers down near the city's front gate, Rahab heard the knock at her door. "Two foreigners were seen entering your house," the officer said. "They're probably spies—send 'em out so we can deal with them."

"I'd love to," she replied. "but they left a couple hours ago. Ride fast, though, and you'll probably catch them on the road."

Off they went in search of the spies—and up Rahab went to her flat roof. "They're gone," she whispered. And out from under sheaves of grain drying on her roof crawled the two spies, who stood up stiffly and brushed themselves off.

"Not sure why you did this," one of them said, "but thanks. Thanks a lot. Anything we can do to repay you?"

And Rahab proposed her price. She didn't want to die when the Israeli army captured her city. And capture it they would, she was certain—for everyone in the province had heard how powerful was Yahweh, the Israelites' God. That Red Sea rumor was still making Canaanite kings nervous, even forty years later. So all Rahab wanted was to be on Yahweh's side when Jericho fell. She and her household, that is.

"Deal," said the spies. And when Israel eventually attacked Jericho, they kept their promise and saved Rahab, her parents, her siblings—everyone in her house. From that day on, she lived among the Jews. In fact, there's reason to think that she married one, and became the mother of Boaz, who when he grew up took a young widow named Ruth to be his wife. But that's another story.

God didn't need a good reason to love Rahab. Neither should we need a good reason to love others. God loved her in spite of her pagan religion, in spite of her immoral lifestyle—loved her only (it seems) because she believed what she heard, and she didn't want to get flattened when judgment arrived.

Can you lavish your love as freely on people like Rahab?

Have Another Helping . . .

Have Another Helping . . .

Y ou've read several Bible verses (if not chapters) in the past week or so. So consider this a Bible-reading Sabbath for yourself: You won't read any new Bible passages today, but you have a chance today to reflect, ruminate, consider, mull, and weigh what you've already read.

In fact, there's even space here to write down anything that's been boiling around in your head or your heart for the past few days. So if you're the writing type, write on.

THOUGHTS

What's making sense to you about all this hunger stuff so far?

What's not making sense?

FEELINGS

How does what you've read so far make you feel? Did anything in the Bible or in the readings stop you in your tracks, fry your brain, or otherwise rearrange how you feel about poverty, hunger, the hungry, and what the Bible says about them all?

QUESTIONS

What questions are still spinning in your head? What's still unclear to you? What questions do you wish you could ask *us*?

DECISION

Recall the previous ten or so readings in this book. (Yes, of course it's okay to flip back and review them now. . . . Finished? Good.) What one act or conversation or meeting can you realistically vow to do—or *start* doing—within the next ten days? The only criterion is that your act or conversation or meeting must in some way, if ever so small, begin to make at least one person or one family or one neighborhood less hungry.

Why The King Adopted A Cripple

> The king then asked him, "Is anyone still alive from Saul's family? If so, I want to show God's kindness to them in any way I can."
>
> Ziba replied, "Yes, one of Jonathan's sons is still alive, but he is crippled."
>
> 2 Samuel 9:3

The idea of loving someone as an obligation may not strike you as sufficiently saintly or righteous. If you don't have warm feelings, after all, does your act of love even *count* as love? If you feel you *ought* to love someone, then you're paying a debt—you aren't really loving, right?

Maybe, maybe not. Consider King David of ancient Israel, who one day remembered how he missed his best friend and soul mate, Jonathan, who had died in battle some time earlier. David wondered aloud if Jonathan had any relatives left that David could show kindness to. There turned out to be one—Mephibosheth, Jonathan's son, who as a five-year-old had been dropped by his nurse while fleeing an enemy assault (2 Samuel 4:4). Mephibosheth was an adult now and still crippled from that fall. David looked him up, and—because of a debt of love David felt he owed Jonathan—pretty much adopted Mephibosheth. He made him a permanent member of David's royal family, giving him his own rooms in the palace and letting him eat meals with him as if he were David's own son.

It is reasonable to assume that David probably developed warm feelings for Mephibosheth, David being the passionate man he was. Yet it wouldn't have mattered. The point was that Mephibosheth's father, Jonathan, had been David's best friend. Jonathan was now dead, the crippled Mephibosheth was down and out, and David could extend his love and care to at least a son of his soul mate, Jonathan, if not to Jonathan himself any more.

This world is full of cripples—people crippled literally and figuratively by chronic hunger, by disease, by poverty, by being so cornered by circumstances that they no longer have any options. You don't have to work up tender or passionate or sympathetic feelings in order to reach out to them with who you are, with what you have. You aren't nearly as hemmed in by circumstances as they are. So reach out and help. There's a least a *little* something you can do to ease their life.

Mothers, Babies, Sword, and Love

Mothers, Babies, Sword, and Love

> Then the woman who really was the mother of the
> living child, and who loved him very much, cried
> out, "Oh no, my lord! Give her the child—please do
> not kill him!"
>
> 1 Kings 3:26

Among the dozens of legal cases that came before King
Solomon that afternoon was a disagreement between two
prostitutes who lived near each other. (You can read the brief
story in the Old Testament, 1 Kings, chapter 3.) Each woman
had very recently given birth to an infant, Solomon learned,
and—as was common then—the mothers slept with their
newborns. Tragically, one mother in her sleep had rolled onto
her baby and killed it. Desperate, the mother tiptoed into the
other woman's room and exchanged babies—took the living
one for her own, and left the dead one in its place.

Each woman claimed to be the mother of the living child
and accused the *other* woman of doing the sneaky switcheroo.
The question for Solomon to answer was, *Which woman
was telling the truth?* Then he'd know who to award the living child to.

"Well," Solomon told the women, "this one is a real
stumper. I have no idea where the truth lies. So what do you

say we simply split the child between both of you."

The court reporter looked up from his notes. "You mean joint custody, right, sire?"

"No," Solomon said, "I mean split the child. Sword, please."

"Sounds fair to me," said one mother.

"No, no, no!" cried the other mother. "Give my baby to her, if it means he will live."

"Okey dokey," said Solomon, putting down the sword. "Now we know who the real mother is. Bailiff, make sure this woman leaves the courtroom with her living son in her arms."

In this story is a good motto to live by, when you consider all that is legally and rightfully yours—and the great need there is in the world. *Give away what is legally and rightfully mine, if it means someone will live.* Several centuries later St. Paul wrote as much to Christians in Ephesus:

> Follow God's example in everything you do, because you are his dear children. Live a life filled with love for others, following the example of Christ, who loved you and gave himself as a sacrifice to take away your sins. And God was pleased, because that sacrifice was like sweet perfume to him. (Ephesians 5:1–2, NLT)

Okay, so now we have *two* examples of giving away what you have if it means saving the life of someone: the ancient mother and Jesus. What more encouragement do you need to open your heart, your wallet, your schedule in order to save the lives of people in dire need in your own country or across the ocean?

The Jewish National Welfare System

The Jewish National Welfare System

> At the end of every third year bring the tithe of
> all your crops and store it in the nearest town.
> Give it to the Levites, who have no inheritance
> among you, as well as to the foreigners living
> among you, the orphans, and the widows in your
> towns, so they can eat and be satisfied. Then the
> LORD your God will bless you in all your work.
>
> Deuteronomy 14:28–29

First, a couple definitions: A *tithe* is a tenth. When God commanded the Jews to tithe, he was commanding them to give him one dove (the best) for every ten doves they owned, or one bushel basket of barley (from the first harvest—the best harvest) for every ten bushel baskets of barley they reaped.

The *Levites* were the priestly family of Israel. After the patriarch Abraham and his son Isaac, it was Isaac's son Jacob (renamed *Israel* by God) who had twelve sons of his own. And these sons grew up to become leaders of their own clans, or families. (You may have heard of the twelve *tribes* of Israel?) Hence, "the children of Israel"—that is, the Jews.

Anyway, Levi was one of those twelve sons of Jacob, and God stipulated that *his* family and descendents (the Levites) would be priests—men and women who served God as intermediaries between him and his people, who represented the people of the nation Israel to God.

When Moses and Joshua led the Jews back to Canaan, unlike the other eleven families, the Levites were given no land they could call their own. "You priests will receive no inheritance of land or share of property among the people of Israel," was how God put it to the descendents of Levi. "I am your inheritance and your share." Instead of farming their nonexistent land, Levites lived off a portion of the *tithes* that all the other Jews brought to the priests.

But only a portion. For some of that tithe went to immigrants, orphans, and widows—individuals who have traditionally been on the socioeconomic fringe in just about any culture. In other cultures such people ended up thieving, selling their bodies for cash, or begging outside Kmart.

Not God's people, though. His vision for a just society included an economic system that took care of those who could not feed themselves. Thanks to the tithes, the poor and vulnerable (that is, the hungry) shared in the harvest that the able-bodied gathered.

There's a little promise attached to God's command to feed the hungry "so that they can eat and be satisfied": God will bless you in all your work.

Don't Be So Efficient!

> When you are harvesting your crops and forget to
> bring in a bundle of grain from your field, don't
> go back to get it. Leave it for the foreigners,
> orphans, and widows. Then the LORD your God will
> bless you in all you do. When you beat the olives
> from your olive trees, don't go over the boughs
> twice. Leave some of the olives for the foreigners,
> orphans, and widows. This also applies to the
> grapes in your vineyard. Do not glean the vines
> after they are picked, but leave any remaining
> grapes for the foreigners, orphans, and widows.
> Remember that you were slaves in the land of
> Egypt. That is why I am giving you this command.
>
> Deuteronomy 24:19–22

Even a skim of the law of Moses gives you the feeling that God
has a big soft spot in his heart for foreigners (immigrants and
aliens), orphans, and widows. The reason is clear: In ancient
times—and generally today, too—these are the people most
vulnerable, least able to provide sufficiently for themselves,
and therefore usually the most needy.

Case in point: Look at God's idea of a just society. Among
other things, you are to give a portion of what you earn to the
poor and the hungry (cash, food, bus fare, whatever). Ancient

Jews were to give an exact proportion—a tenth, or *tithe*, which a lot of Christian churches today require or recommend, usually cash.

So what do we do? Take one tomato out of your bag and leave it on the curb in the parking lot? Swing by the city park on the way home and leave a loaf of bread on a bench?

Of course not. Well, just a minute . . . if you can get over the unusualness of those acts, are they really that far off the mark of what God is asking for even in these modern times?

Okay, let's get a bit less eccentric (remember, though, that saints are usually eccentric) and a little more practical:

- How do we today leave a bit of the harvest out in the fields for the poor, the needy, the hungry?

- Finally, what action can *you* take, what phone calls can *you* make, what emails can *you* send to get the surplus that 80 percent of your society wastes into the homes and mouths of the 20 percent who are poor and hungry?

God's Model For A Just Society

> Suppose this son . . . does not exploit the poor,
> but instead is fair to debtors and does not rob
> them. And suppose this son feeds the hungry,
> provides clothes for the needy, helps the poor,
> does not lend money at interest, and obeys all my
> regulations and laws.
>
> Ezekiel 18:15–17

The economic system that God drafted for ancient Israel took care of those who were on the socioeconomic fringes—those who scraped a living out of poverty, who had no able-bodied worker in the household (like orphans and widows, for example), who had no way to feed themselves, who were chronically hungry.

- *God's economic system forbids taking advantage of poor people in their desperation.* Around a third of U.S. families headed by persons age fifty and older do not have checking accounts. A checking account is even more of a rarity when you're talking about low-income people, older women, and minorities. There are lots of reasons for this: For starters, such people often can't afford a bank's required minimum balances, initial deposits, or monthly fees.

Enter check-cashing outlets, which will gladly cash those Social Security checks and weekly paychecks. Their fee? Ten to twenty percent of the amount of the check. Do the math: to cash a $500 check, the outlets keep $50 to $75 (and higher) out of that check. Check-cashing outlets know that poor people often have nowhere else to go in order to cash a check—and this is plain, old-fashioned exploitation.

- *God's economic system is fair to debtors . . . does not rob them . . . does not lend money at interest.* God's economic system makes sure that if you borrow money, you pay it back—but not with a punishing interest rate so high that you can make scarcely any headway on repaying the principal. True, God's economic system isn't intended to bail you out after running up a $5,000 bill at Bloomingdales. But God never intended his people to be ground down while loan companies get fat off your interest.

- *God's economic system feeds the hungry.* It has always, and in nearly every culture, been a virtue to feed the hungry, however you do it—these days, by donating canned food, buying a poor and hungry guy a hamburger, or by passing legislation that provides for the hungry.

So where does this all leave you?

- Those on the lower rungs of our socioeconomic system usually rent their homes instead of buying them. So how affordable is rental housing for poor people in your area? What rent controls, if any, are in place in your town?

- Does a person's interest or even passion about such things make her an *activist* or a *biblical Christian*? Is there a difference?

Real Prisoners, Real Blindness, Real Hunger

[God] gives justice to the oppressed and food to
    the hungry.
The LORD frees the prisoners.
The LORD opens the eyes of the blind.
The LORD lifts the burdens of those bent beneath
    their loads.
The LORD loves the righteous.
The LORD protects the foreigners among us.
He cares for the orphans and widows, but he
    frustrates the plans of the wicked.

Psalm 146:7–9

Many Christian churches have spent so many years *spiritualizing* verses like these that they have all but lost touch with the literal meaning of the words.

Case in point: The Lord frees the prisoners, you often hear, from the chains of *sin*. The Lord opens the eyes of those who are blind—*spiritually* blind, that is, before they get saved. The Lord lifts burdens—burdens of *sin*, of course. The Lord gives food to the hungry—those who hunger for the *truth*, that is; and the food that satisfies that hunger is the meat of the Bible, the Word of God.

Hey, metaphors are great. The Bible is full of them.

But what about verses (like those above) that make plenty of sense literally, before plunging into what they *could* mean figuratively? For example, what if God was not only The Lord Who Frees Us from the Prison of Sin, but also The Lord Who Frees Actual Jailbirds and Convicts? Even if you're convinced that every prisoner in the U.S. is a criminal and behind bars justly, heaven knows there are many thousands of political prisoners in the world—incarcerated women and men—who were locked up for nothing more than voicing their disagreement with their governments. Not for disobeying their governments' laws, but merely for voicing *disagreement* with those laws. How long has it been since you've prayed not "to you, Lord, who frees us from sin and feeds us with your Word" but "to you, Lord, who frees prisoners wrongly imprisoned, who puts food on the table of the hungry"?

All of this means, quite possibly, that Christians are servants of a Lord who protect immigrants and aliens (legal, illegal—does it matter?), protect single parents struggling on two minimum-wage jobs, protects migrant workers or mentally disabled persons so poor that they can't even afford the *deposit* on a rental house in a safe part of town. What if we serve a Lord whose heart's desires include bringing justice to the oppressed and feeding the hungry?

And what if we are the only hands God has to accomplish his heart's desire among our society's throwaway people?

Then Boaz asked his foreman, "Who is that girl over there?"

And the foreman replied, "She is the young woman from Moab who came back with Naomi. She asked me this morning if she could gather grain behind the harvesters. She has been hard at work ever since, except for a few minutes' rest over there in the shelter."

Boaz went over and said to Ruth, "Listen, my daughter. Stay right here with us when you gather grain; don't go to any other fields. Stay right behind the women working in my field. See which part of the field they are harvesting, and then follow them. I have warned the young men not to bother you. And when you are thirsty, help yourself to the water they have drawn from the well."

Ruth fell at his feet and thanked him warmly. "Why are you being so kind to me?" she asked. "I am only a foreigner."

When Ruth went back to work again, Boaz ordered his young men, "Let her gather grain right among the sheaves without stopping her. And pull out some heads of barley from the bundles and drop

them on purpose for her. Let her pick them up, and
don't give her a hard time!"

Ruth 2:5—10, 15—16

The story of Ruth and Boaz is most of all a love story. But it's
a love story in a context of widowhood, poverty, and
hunger. In ancient times women without men were usually
taken advantage of—financially and sexually, among other
ways. It was no wonder that young women like Ruth typically became prostitutes so they could at least eat with the
cash they earned from their services. (It is the same today,
particularly in developing countries whose bleak economies
offer no legitimate jobs to unattached women with children
to support.)

But if Ruth was reduced to scavenging on the fields behind
the harvesting crews, they were at least the fields of a relative of her deceased father-in-law. And if Boaz did nothing
else righteous in his life, he did this one good thing: He made
sure that his harvesting crews didn't give her a hard time as
she picked up the mere leftovers of the barley crop—which
was exactly what God had been telling the Jews all along:
"Take care of the needy! Let your surplus feed them! Even if
you have no surplus, share what you have with the hungry!"

Which is what God is still telling us today.

Yet what does today's society think of people who
scrounge for leftovers, like Ruth did in the ancient barley
fields of Boaz? How do you stereotype them? How can

today's poor and hungry—the poor and hungry in *your* town—get enough food without scrounging?

It has been said that poverty is not a lack of money, but a lack of options. What do you think about this definition? If you had no food in your cupboards or pantry or basement or freezer, how would you eat? Let us guess: With three bucks you'd find lying around your room in change—or that you'd get from your mom's purse—you'd go grab a McChicken sandwich and fries. Now compare that to a poor person who must choose to spend her last ten bucks either on a minimum payment to the utility company to keep the electricity on and her house warm, or on food. What options do you have when you're hungry? What options does a poor person have when he is hungry?

Last questions:

- What kind of scrounging—or, to use the ancient picture, "field gleaning"—could *you* do for the poor and the hungry?

- What stores would donate food that is too old to sell but still good? How would you ask them?

- If stores would give you their old food, where would you take it? How would you distribute it? What agencies are already up and running in your community that do this sort of thing? How could you assist their efforts?

Let My People Eat!

"We have fasted before you!" they say. "Why aren't you impressed? We have done much penance, and you don't even notice it!"

I will tell you why! It's because you are living for yourselves even while you are fasting. You keep right on oppressing your workers. What good is fasting when you keep on fighting and quarreling? This kind of fasting will never get you anywhere with me.

No, the kind of fasting I want calls you to free those who are wrongly imprisoned and to stop oppressing those who work for you. Treat them fairly and give them what they earn. I want you to share your food with the hungry and to welcome poor wanderers into your homes. Give clothes to those who need them, and do not hide from relatives who need your help.

Stop oppressing the helpless and stop making false accusations and spreading vicious rumors! Feed the hungry and help those in trouble. Then your light will shine out from the darkness, and the darkness around you will be as bright as day.

Isaiah 58:3–4, 6–8, 9–10

Truth comes in pairs, it has been said. For example, it is very, very true that spiritual realities are eternally crucial—like salvation, like heaven or hell, like if a person does or doesn't accept Jesus as their Savior.

But there's the other half of this truth which, unfortunately, though equally important, hasn't gotten nearly as much air time in many churches. It's this: As critical as spiritual realities are, taking care of others' *bodies* is just as important to God as tending their souls.

And that explains why God ripped into his people Israel for abandoning his economic model. As urgent and eternally important as salvation is, God makes it excruciatingly clear in passages like this one in Isaiah 58 that he is immensely concerned with the physical well-being of the poor, the hungry, the needy, the marginalized. Treat them bad, and you might as well spit in God's face.

You could say, in fact, that God went ballistic on the ancient affluent exactly because they didn't get this truth-comes-in-pairs stuff. If you had asked any of them, "Are you obeying God? Are you attending to your spiritual lives?" they would have said—well, read for yourself what they *did* say: "Hey, we have fasted! Gone without food for extended periods of time, all so we could hear your voice, God, and obey you better! We have sacrificed ourselves in so many ways, deprived ourselves of money and sleep, not to mention food. What more do you want, God?"

"Glad you asked," you can almost hear God respond. "For starters, attend to the physical welfare of the poor as much as you do to the spiritual growth of yourselves. Stop paying your entry-level employees poverty wages, telling yourself it's more than they'd get anywhere else. Pay a wage they can live on. And you landlords, stop raising the rents on your mediocre properties just because the market will bear it.

"Figure out ways to make housing affordable for poor people who have had neither the opportunities to go to college nor the required connections to get a good job. Figure out ways to share your food with the hungry. Treat your employees fairly, even if it means dinging your bottom line some. If you sacrifice in stuff like this as well as in your fasting and religious stuff, I'll make sure your lights shine brightly. I'll take care of you."

When God Hates Worship

When God Hates Worship

> You trample the poor and steal what little they
> have through taxes and unfair rent.
>
> I hate all your show and pretense—the hypocrisy
> of your religious festivals and solemn assemblies.
> I will not accept your burnt offerings and grain
> offerings. I won't even notice all your choice
> peace offerings. Away with your hymns of praise!
> They are only noise to my ears. I will not listen
> to your music, no matter how lovely it is. Instead,
> I want to see a mighty flood of justice, a river
> of righteous living that will never run dry.
>
> Amos 5:11a, 21–24

You walk through your church's lobby and into the sanctuary—and whether it's a high-ceilinged stone cathedral with morning sun streaming through stained glass or a sleek auditorium equipped with concert lighting and video projection, you're ready to worship. The pre-service mood may be quietly meditative or a happy chattiness, but you're there and you're ready to focus on God and sing hymns with everyone and offer up your sacrifice of praise and, when the offering plate is passed, a little cash, too.

Did you know that, under some circumstances, God *hates* this?

47

God steps on a lot of toes here—ours as well as the toes of the ancient Jews, to whom he was directly speaking. Worship services, religious assemblies, offerings, worship music—all the stuff you'd expect God to applaud, he said he hated. *Hated*.

And why? Because even some of the affluent who attend church faithfully and sing praises to God and give their generous offerings to church collections walk out of church and back into their offices on Monday morning to grind down the poor into hopelessness with taxes, unfair rents, and oppressive working conditions. And in the process, they drive these poor deeper and deeper into hunger and need.

Consider the case of Sodom—you know, the ancient city that was destroyed by fire and brimstone for the people's wickedness. We get some specifics in Ezekiel 16:49 about what that wickedness was all about: The sin of Sodom, the prophet wrote, was the city's "pride, laziness, and gluttony, while the poor and needy suffered outside her door."

Having plenty to eat themselves but never using a portion of it to feed the hungry poor all around them. Sound familiar?

- Do you see anything like this going on today? In what instances might you, your youth group, your church, or your denomination be on the verge of paying more attention to worship than to taking care of the poor and the hungry?

- Is God saying here that we should take care of the poor and hungry *instead* of worship?

Simply Compassion

> Then Jesus called his disciples to him and said,
> "I feel sorry for these people. They have been
> here with me for three days, and they have nothing
> left to eat. I don't want to send them away
> hungry, or they will faint along the road."

Matthew 15:32

Flip your Bible open to any of the Gospels (that would be the first four books of the New Testament—Matthew, Mark, Luke, or John), and chances are you can't read two chapters without encountering a healing. The Gospels teem with healings. And after you read a bunch of them, you realize that:

- When people were hungry, Jesus fed them—no questions asked.

- When Jesus gave new legs to a lifelong cripple, he didn't first ask him, "Are you an observant Jew? Did you read your Torah verses during morning devotions today? You did? Good . . . then I'll heal you now . . ."

- Jesus healed blindness without afterwards requiring the fresh-sighted person to join the local synagogue.

In short, Jesus didn't heal people in order to "get them saved" or to make some spiritual point. He healed them because the blind and crippled and diseased were among the lowest socioeconomic class in Judah, which meant they lived in substandard housing, usually begged for a living, and if disease didn't start them down this road to poverty and hunger, it would likely follow. He healed these poor and hungry people simply because he felt compassion for them. (Granted, a lot of individuals whom Jesus healed became his followers, but that was a choice they made, not a condition Jesus made for healing them.)

Take a look at Matthew 15:29–39, when Jesus fed four thousand people at one time. (If you're wondering if it wasn't five thousand Jesus fed like this, you're right: on another occasion he did indeed feed five thousand with five loaves of bread and a pair of fish—read about *that* in Matthew 14:13–21. But at this event it was a mere four thousand, seven loaves, and "a few small fish." Which goes to show that when people were hungry, Jesus didn't mind at all doing sequels.)

How long had this crowd been without food? What was Jesus' motivation for providing food for them?

Does it strike you as curious that these people were getting miraculously healed right and left but that when Jesus saw that they were *hungry* that's when he felt sorry for them?

What does this Bible narrative tell you about your own sense of compassion? What sort of things arouse your sympathy? In what ways, if any, should your sympathy be broadened to include more than it does?

Have Another Helping . . .

Have Another Helping . . .

Y ou've read several Bible verses (if not chapters) in the past week or so. So consider this a Bible-reading Sabbath for yourself: You won't read any new Bible passages today, but you have a chance today to reflect, ruminate, consider, mull, and weigh what you've already read.

In fact, there's even space here to write down anything that's been boiling around in your head or your heart for the past few days. So if you're the writing type, write on.

THOUGHTS

What's making sense to you about all this hunger stuff so far?

What's not making sense?

FEELINGS

How does what you've read so far make you feel? Did anything in the Bible or in the readings stop you in your tracks, fry your brain, or otherwise rearrange how you feel about poverty, hunger, the hungry, and what the Bible says about them all?

QUESTIONS

What questions are still spinning in your head? What's still unclear to you? What questions do you wish you could ask *us*?

DECISION

Recall the previous ten or so readings in this book. (Yes, of course it's okay to flip back and review them now. . . . Finished? Good.) What one act or conversation or meeting can you realistically vow to do—or *start* doing—within the next ten days? The only criterion is that your act or conversation or meeting must in some way, if ever so small, begin to make at least one person or one family or one neighborhood less hungry.

What Some People
Will Do for a Meal . . .

What Some People
Will Do for a Meal . . .

One day when Jacob was cooking some stew, Esau
arrived home exhausted and hungry from a hunt.
Esau said to Jacob, "I'm starved! Give me some of
that red stew you've made." (This was how Esau got
his other name, Edom—"Red.")

Jacob replied, "All right, but trade me your
birthright for it."

"Look, I'm dying of starvation!" said Esau.
"What good is my birthright to me now?"

So Jacob insisted, "Well then, swear to me
right now that it is mine." So Esau swore an oath,
thereby selling all his rights as the firstborn to
his younger brother.

Then Jacob gave Esau some bread and lentil
stew. Esau ate and drank and went on about his
business, indifferent to the fact that he had
given up his birthright.

Genesis 25:29–34

History has been way too hard on Esau. Open just about any
reading or study about the very different twins Jacob and
Esau and, more often than not, Esau gets slammed and
Jacob gets praised. It all sounds too much like a scene from

Of Mice and Men: Esau a big, hairy lunk on the dense side and Jacob the wiry, crafty, barely younger twin who got all the brains.

Yet maybe we're too harsh. Maybe Esau wasn't quite as big a doofus as he's made out to be. A typical day's actions and decisions—even your thoughts—are influenced less by cold logic and calm wisdom than by your plain old mammalian urges and appetites. The hunger that comes from a delayed lunch during a downtown shopping trip makes you grumpy with your sister.

You can vow, you can resolve, you can determine—but your body often ends up calling the shots. Sometimes that's good, sometimes it's destructive. It's called being human. We may have souls, but those souls are housed in animal bodies. Our bodies are our glory and our shame. With our bodies we worship God; with our bodies we sense the fullness of the world and each other that God has given us. And with our bodies, we can destroy ourselves and each other if we want.

Like hunger. Food. Stew. Esau was just like us, liable to a moment's hissy fit and rash decision because his stomach was growling.

No wonder Jesus usually fed the hungry and healed the diseased before he preached to them. He knew that the human body is a sacred, powerful thing, a road into the spirit. First things first.

Where Famine Drives People

When Jacob heard that there was grain available in
Egypt, he said to his sons, "Why are you standing
around looking at one another? I have heard there
is grain in Egypt. Go down and buy some for us
before we all starve to death." So Joseph's ten
older brothers went down to Egypt to buy grain.

Genesis 42:1–3

Revealing the end of Joseph's story won't spoil the telling for
you—there's plenty of intrigue, executions, mistaken identi-
ties, and blackmail along the way. The two-sentence summary is this: A famine moved the people of Israel from
Canaan to Egypt. And unknown to the starving Israelites,
God had plopped Joseph down in Egypt years earlier in order
to aid his estranged family when they needed food and
needed it badly.

Tragically, the famine part of the story has been repeated
many thousands of times since then, and is being retold even
today. Where hasn't the bite of famine been felt? And
whereas famine has traditionally been the result of drought,
flood, insect plagues, or war, famines these days are intensi-
fied by economic forces that are global in scale.

It should be enough to know that, according to the United

Nations World Food Program, "every day malnutrition is a significant factor in the deaths of eleven thousand children." That's right: Somewhere in the world, one child dies every eight seconds.*

Famine drives parents in India to sell their children who become indentured servants and slaves for their owners (yes, it happens even today). Famine drives Rwandan mothers to sell their bodies on the street in order to feed their children.

And famine drove the aging Jacob and his eleven sons (and their sizable families) to Egypt and its famine-relief administrator, upon whom they knew they were utterly dependent. The administrator, it turned out happily, was their long-lost brother Joseph—the one person in the world who could deal graciously with them, who could provide for them, who could meet their starving need.

Has it occurred to you that God may have planted you where you are now, and in this time, in order to meet the starving need of someone in your town, your state, your hemisphere, your world? If one is to conclude anything from the Bible, it is that God is in the business of arranging some people to help meet the needs of other people.

Famine drives people to desperation, to migration—and to *you*.

*From United Nations World Food Program,
http://www.wfp.org/index.asp?section=1

Did They Even Deserve Manna?

They arrived a month after leaving Egypt. There, too, the whole community of Israel spoke bitterly against Moses and Aaron.

"Oh, that we were back in Egypt," they moaned. "It would have been better if the LORD had killed us there! At least there we had plenty to eat. But now you have brought us into this desert to starve us to death."

The next morning the desert all around the camp was wet with dew. When the dew disappeared later in the morning, thin flakes, white like frost, covered the ground. The Israelites were puzzled when they saw it. "What is it?" they asked.

And Moses told them, "It is the food the LORD has given you. The LORD says that each household should gather as much as it needs. Pick up two quarts for each person."

So the people of Israel went out and gathered this food—some getting more, and some getting less. By gathering two quarts for each person, everyone had just enough. Those who gathered a lot had nothing left over, and those who gathered only a little had enough. Each family had just what it needed.

Exodus 16:1–3, 13–18

Under Moses' leadership, the million or so people of Israel had left Egypt only a month earlier. Now they were in the desert—no water, no food. At least in Egypt, they complained to each other, there was plenty of food, even if they lived as slaves. Irrigated by the Nile's waters, the Hebrews' fields abounded with crops.

God hears their complaints, feels their hunger, and so gives them—well, this *stuff*. The first morning they found it on the ground they asked, "What *is* it?" In Hebrew, their language, you say, "What *is* it?" like this: "Man-na." And so this became the name of this edible whatever-it-was. Manna.

Judging from this story, you don't have to be a saint, a Christian, or even a particularly good person to get from God what you need, food or otherwise. Just look at the griping and belly-aching Israel did—with some accusations against Yahweh thrown in for emphasis. (Read the chapters on either side of Exodus 16, too, for even *more* griping they did.) Yet God didn't hold back because of their attitude, but granted them what he apparently thought was their legitimate request: It was a desert, they had no food, they were hungry. It appears that under such circumstances, God doesn't have a lot of spiritual requirements before he blesses people. Like Jesus said, God "gives his sunlight to both the evil and the good, and he sends rain on the just and on the unjust, too" (Matthew 5:45).

This episode from the Bible should confirm what common sense and our observation tell us: that the gift of food is not contingent on the godliness of the hungry. Pagans, animists, atheists, heretics, Protestants, Catholics, charismatics, Mormons—when any one of us is hungry and cries out for food, the heart of God is moved. His desire is to feed. Of course, God's desire is *also* for a person to surrender to God's saving grace. But that seems to be God's desire, not condition.

When Jesus healed the maimed and diseased during those three brief terrestrial years, it is not recorded that he first asked if they were regular attenders at synagogue. He did not require a notarized itemization of their tithes and offerings. All Jesus said was things like, "Do you want to be healed?" or "Do you believe I can heal you?" or "Go home! You're healed, already!"

What hoops do *you* want people to jump through when they tell you they're hungry? The homeless person on the downtown street corner who asks for spare change? The Latino kid at school whose parents, are migrant field workers, and who wears the same clothes several days a week, and who eats a bag of chips for lunch every day? The faces of the starving in Asia and Africa that you see in magazines? Are you requiring more of them than God does before you feed them?

No! Not the Holy Bread!

"Now, [David said,] what is there to eat? Give me
five loaves of bread or anything else you have."

"We don't have any regular bread," the priest
replied. "But there is the holy bread."

So, since there was no other food available, the
priest gave him the holy bread—the Bread of the
Presence that was placed before the LORD in the
Tabernacle. It had just been replaced that day
with fresh bread.

1 Samuel 21:3–4, 6

King Saul's manic jealousy of David had finally forced the giant killer and court musician to flee for his life. Alone, hungry, weaponless, and homeless, the young fugitive went to a priest he knew, lied about being on a secret mission for the king, and asked for food for himself and his supposed troops waiting for him outside the city.

It is often surprising to modern readers that the priest offered David the holy bread. Whoa, the holy bread? The stuff that sat on a special table in the Holy Place of the tabernacle and, later, of the temple? The priest gave David *that* to eat?

It's enough to make you wonder what *holy* means, anyway.

Glad you asked: The Hebrew word for *holy* carries the idea of being set apart, reserved for a special use. All the fur-

60

niture and food in Israel's temple was holy in that it was set apart for a particular use: that is, God's use. The crackers or bread down in the kitchen that you use for communion. The baptismal font or baptistery that holds water for baptisms. These items are not humans-cannot-touch-this holy, but only reserved-for-special-use holy.

So the priest evidently judged that David's hunger was as holy a purpose for the special temple bread as to leave it sit there.

In case people didn't get it, Jesus hammered the idea home several centuries later:

> One Sabbath day as Jesus was walking through some grainfields, his disciples began breaking off heads of wheat. But the Pharisees said to Jesus, "They shouldn't be doing that! It's against the law to work by harvesting grain on the Sabbath."
>
> But Jesus replied, "Haven't you ever read in the Scriptures what King David did when he and his companions were hungry? He went into the house of God (during the days when Abiathar was high priest), ate the special bread reserved for the priests alone, and then gave some to his companions. That was breaking the law, too." Then he said to them, "The Sabbath was made to benefit people, and not people to benefit the Sabbath." (Mark 2:23–27)

Bottom line: It's your hunger that sanctifies food—that makes it holy. The hunger of people next door or across the county line or in another continent sanctifies whatever food you give them, directly or indirectly. This is holy work, this giving of food to people who are hungry.

You May Be the Fairytale Answer to Someone's Hunger

You May Be the Fairytale Answer to Someone's Hunger

But [the widow] said, "I swear by the LORD your God that I don't have a single piece of bread in the house. And I have only a handful of flour left in the jar and a little cooking oil in the bottom of the jug. I was just gathering a few sticks to cook this last meal, and then my son and I will die."

But Elijah said to her, "Don't be afraid! Go ahead and cook that `last meal,' but bake me a little loaf of bread first. Afterward there will still be enough food for you and your son. For this is what the LORD, the God of Israel, says: There will always be plenty of flour and oil left in your containers until the time when the LORD sends rain and the crops grow again!"

1 Kings 17:12–14

If only this would happen over the cooking fires in Zambia's shantytowns . . . in the rice pots of starving farmers in Bangladesh . . . in the kitchens of Memphis and Montreal and Ciudad Juarez, where people are still out of work after a year of job hunting. Why were this unnamed widow and her son miraculously saved from starvation, and many millions of people since then—including a lot of Christians—*not* saved? Where are God's miracles when millions of Ethiopians and Afghanis in our own time slowly die by starvation?

It's a tough nut to crack. Start talking about this, and before you know it you're talking about the nature of God, the source of evil, and the intersection of God's will and human choices.

Maybe part of the answer lies in why Elijah went to the widow in the first place. "Go and live in the village of Zarephath, near the city of Sidon," God had told him. "There is a widow there who will feed you. I have given her my instructions" (1 Kings 17: 9). Maybe the widow would have appreciated knowing those instructions earlier in time, rather than merely watching her flour urn get lighter and lighter, while she got more and more desperate. In any case, God prepped Elijah to relieve the hunger of this woman and her son.

Is it possible that God is prepping you, speaking to you, nudging your spirit, or otherwise getting your attention about feeding someone? Someone near, someone far . . . someone you know, someone you know about, someone you've never thought of before?

The Way to His Heart Was through
His Stomach—Even for Jesus

The Way to His Heart Was through His Stomach—Even for Jesus

> Then Jesus was led out into the wilderness by the
> Holy Spirit to be tempted there by the Devil. For
> forty days and forty nights he ate nothing and
> became very hungry. Then the Devil came and said
> to him, "If you are the Son of God, change these
> stones into loaves of bread."
>
> But Jesus told him, "No! The Scriptures say,
> 'People need more than bread for their life; they
> must feed on every word of God.'"
>
> Matthew 4:1–4

Today's Word of the Day is *gnosticism*. Simply and very generally (if you want details, go to Google), it's a belief that stuff is bad and spirit is good. This is because, gnostics believe, God is spirit and is good. The opposite of spirit is matter, so matter must be evil.

This is an old, old belief that keeps popping up in every era. That's gnosticism you're hearing any time you hear people say some *thing*—some physical object or substance—is evil, regardless of the use one makes of it.

Gnosticism shows up in subtle ways, too—whenever, in fact, people suspect that something God *created* is sinful.

Chances are, however, the book or herb or pork loin aren't evil—it's the gluttony or obsession or self-destructive *use* of these things that's evil.

So along comes Jesus, fasting in the desert, probably hungrier than he had ever been, and the devil tempts him with the possibility of a meal. Notice that Jesus did not say, "People don't need bread for life—they need the Word of God." He said, in essence, "People need bread for life; everyone knows that. Beyond that, though, everyone needs the Word of God, too."

Like any human, Jesus needed both. It was just a matter of timing as to which he had at what time. He went to the desert to feast not on bread, but on his Father (so to speak). He eventually broke his fast and even feasted at the homes of supposed sinners.

"Everything is pure to those whose hearts are pure," wrote St. Paul to his pastor friend Titus (1:15). Food is not bad, even in comparison to purely spiritual things, like eternal life and salvation and discipleship. Jesus *really needed* food during his thirty-three years on this earth as a human—not more nor less than he needed his Father's spiritual sustenance, but *alongside* it.

Moral: Don't dare think that the food you provide for hungry persons is less important than the gospel you may want to share with them, too. They're both critical. In fact, the odds are they won't think much about spiritual realities until their physical needs are met. That's just the way things are.

What Do You Have?

What Do You Have?

> The disciples replied, "And where would we get enough food out here in the wilderness for all of them to eat?"
>
> Jesus asked, "How many loaves of bread do you have?"

Matthew 15:33–34

Ask anyone on the street for a specific miracle that Jesus did, and odds are fifty-fifty that you'll hear about Jesus feeding a crowd. (The other one will probably be about healing a blind man.)

The Bible records two instances of Jesus feeding a crowd with way, way too little food to start with. The episode described in Matthew 15 involved the feeding of four thousand men, not counting women and children. Say eight thousand to ten thousand at the very least.

And notice that all Jesus wanted to know from his disciples was, "What do you have?" not, "Have you contracted with a food-service provider to feed an arena crowd of ten thousand?" or, "Do you have the logistics in place to cart in food for ten thousand?" Only "What do you have right now?"—with the implication, "Good—then that's what we'll use to get this job done."

When the disciples emptied their backpacks, they counted seven loaves of bread and a few cans of sardines. No wonder they were a tad incredulous and even skeptical. "So let's get this straight, Jesus," they said. "You want to feed ten thousand people. Out here in the sticks. Not a Falafel Bell in sight. Are you serious?"

Yes, Jesus was serious and, yes, the hungry were fed even with the little that was at hand.

So what is in *your* hand to feed the hungry around you, or around the world? It doesn't take much to make a difference. For example:

- For $15 you can buy a blanket for a kid who needs one.

- For $25 you can buy health-care provisions for a child: mosquito net, emergency care, and medicine.

- For $30 you can buy two dairy goats (for milk, cheese, yogurt).

Or you can send any amount you want—a couple bucks, a couple hundred bucks—to feed a child in Iraq, to clothe a family in Liberia, to give medical treatments to infants in Bolivia.

Or are you up for dropping some coin for the hungry *every month*? Even being this regular about it, it doesn't take much— especially for a group of you. For $25 to $30 each month, for instance, you can sponsor a child in a developing country who needs food, clothing, education, and encouragement. Here are the sorts of things a monthly check will do for a child:

- Education assistance
- Opportunities for a child to develop numerous life skills
- Medical checkups, support, and supplemental nutrition as needed
- Ways to develop the child's self-confidence and social skills
- Personal visits from agency's staff or representatives

So hop to it! Check out the Web sites of these organizations (and of any others that you hear about), choose one to deal with, decide what you can send—and send it.

- World Vision (worldvision.org)
- Compassion International (compassion.com)
- Food for the Hungry (fh.org)
- Apathy Is Lethal (apathyislethal.org), a project of UNAIDS, the Joint United Nations Programme on HIV/AIDS (unaids.org)

Luxurious Living

> There was a certain rich man who was splendidly
> clothed and who lived each day in luxury. At his
> door lay a diseased beggar named Lazarus. As Lazarus
> lay there longing for scraps from the rich man's
> table, the dogs would come and lick his open sores.
>
> Luke 16:19–21

The way Jesus told this story makes it sound like just another of his parables. But don't jump to conclusions, some theologians remind us. They point out that in not one of Jesus' parables are any actors identified by proper names. Here, however, the beggar has a name—Lazarus. Which means this may be a true story, the details of which only Jesus was capable of knowing.

Fictitious anecdote or a slice of real life (and death, as you'll see if you read the entire story in Luke 16:19–25), it is not a particularly happy story if you are among the world's minority—that is, if you have plenty to eat. The poor, hungry, diseased beggar, Lazarus, ended up coddled in the comforts of heaven, while the unnamed rich man burned in Hades.

This is all a bit disturbing to most of us, because, well, let's face it: Compared to most of the world, *we* are the rich man. We in the industrialized West. Much of Europe and North

America (though by no means *all* of it) and conspicuous pockets of the Pacific Rim (Tokyo, Hong Kong, Singapore, Sydney) are not chronically hungry. We are rich and splendidly clothed, and we live each day in what to most of the world is utter luxury. Our idea of going without is a year with no vacation. Hardship is the company deducting health-insurance premiums from your paycheck instead of paying them itself. Not having enough clothes means having to wear the same top twice in one week. To lack food means having to fast-food it because you can't make it home for dinner between two appointments. To be hungry means to skip breakfast or lunch in order to lose weight.

Meanwhile, fully half the children in many African countries go to bed hungry every night, wake up hungry every morning, and cannot remember when they felt full after a meal. They are chronically malnourished.

Such children and their parents, if they live near cities, dumpster-dive for whatever scraps they can find. In Latin America, virtual villages spring up around the fringes of urban landfills, where the hungry poor find what they can to survive. They are the modern Lazaruses.

And like it or not, we are the rich men and women, in whose power it is to find a way to feed the hungry or to let them starve.

"Come Have Breakfast"

> When they landed, they saw a fire of burning coals
> there with fish on it, and some bread. Jesus said
> to them, "Come have breakfast."
>
> John 21:9,12, NIV

It wasn't as if Jesus hadn't been breaking in his disciples to the idea that he really was alive again. After his death by crucifixion, he had appeared to them a couple of times already—visibly wounded but otherwise walking, talking, alive, and well. "Never felt better," Jesus told them.

As welcome as this whole resurrection thing was to his followers, though, it was still a little spooky. Was it *really* him? And the way he'd suddenly just *be* there in a room with you, without entering it . . . you'd think he taught apparating at Hogswart or something.

This time they were out fishing—at least those of his disciples who were fishermen—and had had a lousy night at it. Hadn't caught a thing. Not one fish. Nada. Zip. The eastern sky began lightening some as morning twilight began, when they heard a voice and saw a person's silhouette on the beach.

"How's fishing?" the voice shouted over the water.

The disciples grimaced. The last thing they needed was

71

some insomniac villager who wanted to talk over a few hundred yards of water. "Nothing!" they shouted back.

"Try the other side!" the man shouted. Hmmm, thought the disciples. Maybe he was another fisherman who knew something they didn't. So they hauled up their (empty) nets from the left side of the boat, and dropped them over the gunwales on the right. They waited a few minutes, then started hauling them in—and instantly realized that the nets held so many fish, they couldn't haul them all into the boat, but would have to tow the nets to shore.

That was all the clue they needed. The twilight was fading, and they got a better look at the man. "It's the Lord!" Peter exclaimed as he dove in and started swimming to shore. The rest of them hit the oars and steered to the beach. As the boat's keel ground into the sand and the disciples hopped out, Jesus said, "Oh, yeah—bring some of that fish with you. I don't think I have enough for you here." It was then they noticed a small cooking fire at Jesus' feet, with a half-dozen fish grilling and some flat bread warming along the edge of the fire.

"Come and have breakfast," Jesus said.

Jesus never took food or eating lightly. What you ate, where the food came from, who you ate with—you get the feeling that it was all almost sacred. Which it kind of is. It is a gift from the earth, and when we prepare it for ourselves and others it can become a sacrament.

How can we not somehow share this sacrament with others, for whom it is less sacrament and more stark survival?

Feeding Jesus

Feeding Jesus

> "Lord, when did we ever see you hungry and feed
> you?"
>
> And the King will tell them, "I assure you,
> when you did it to one of the least of these my
> brothers and sisters, you were doing it to me!"
>
> Matthew 25:37, 40

The Case of the Disguised Deity. It was never a Nancy Drew
mystery, but it's been one of the most told, if not most
published, series in history. Zeus as a wandering beggar among
mortal villagers, or as a virile bull to abduct and seduce a
human virgin. Or a Hindu god taking tiger form, a Pawnee god
assuming the body of a buffalo, an Egyptian god as a human
pharaoh. Or, in an infernal switch, the devil as an American
lawyer, arguing a case against the upright Daniel Webster.

And, of course, the original from which all these cultural
photocopies were made: Yahweh as a hungry visitor at
Abraham's tent flap, and again, centuries later, as Jesus of
Nazareth.

Ancient peoples (and even modern ones unaffected by the
European Enlightenment) never were too skeptical about this
god-in-human-clothing stuff. They had plenty of stories about
this sort of thing happening, and in fact they could probably

tell you a time or two when they or someone they knew had had an encounter with a disguised deity. So the idea of Jehovah God becoming a man—complete with callused hands, a cowlick, and morning breath—was as likely to first-century Greeks and Romans as a man on the moon is to us.

Trapped in a human body, even gods become hungry. And the God of Abraham, Isaac, and Jacob—in the body of Jesus of Nazareth—was no different. He needed protein and liquids like the next mortal. In fact, he implied, you could divide everyone into two groups: people who gave him food (or drink or clothes or hospitality) and consequently received eternal life, and people who didn't and consequently were deprived of eternal life. Well duh, said his disciples—who *wouldn't* take care of you if salvation was on the line?

You'd be surprised, Jesus said with a wry grin. The out-of-work father who needs a hot meal for his family, the minimum-wage road crew worker in August who looks like he could use a drink, the nineteen-year-old in prison for theft, the single mom whose kids need school clothes that fit them—when you feed, water, visit, or clothe them, you're feeding, watering, visiting, and clothing *Jesus* himself. And if you walk on by these hungry and needy people with less than you, Jesus said (looking serious now), you're ignoring me.

Sometimes you never know exactly who that hungry person you're feeding really is.

Have Another Helping . . .

Have Another Helping . . .

You've read several Bible verses (if not chapters) in the past week or so. So consider this a Bible-reading Sabbath for yourself: You won't read any new Bible passages today, but you have a chance today to reflect, ruminate, consider, mull, and weigh what you've already read.

In fact, there's even space here to write down anything that's been boiling around in your head or your heart for the past few days. So if you're the writing type, write on.

THOUGHTS

What's making sense to you about all this hunger stuff so far?

What's not making sense?

FEELINGS

How does what you've read so far make you feel? Did anything in the Bible or in the readings stop you in your tracks, fry your brain, or otherwise rearrange how you feel about poverty, hunger, the hungry, and what the Bible says about them all?

QUESTIONS

What questions are still spinning in your head? What's still unclear to you? What questions do you wish you could ask *us*?

DECISION

Recall the previous ten or so readings in this book. (Yes, of course it's okay to flip back and review them now. . . . Finished? Good.) What one act or conversation or meeting can you realistically vow to do—or *start* doing—within the next ten days? The only criterion is that your act or conversation or meeting must in some way, if ever so small, begin to make at least one person or one family or one neighborhood less hungry.

Aging and Eating

> And now, in my old age, don't set me aside. Don't
> abandon me when my strength is failing.
>
> Psalm 71:9

You know how, when your family visits grandparents or other older relatives, your parents hang around and talk forever. Way longer than they need to. You're sitting around bored; you gradually migrate to the car where you wait for *another* half-hour before conversation finally winds down with the old folks.

Contrary to adolescent lore, parents don't do this to deliberately drive you to death by boredom. It just happens to turn out that way.

The Bible doesn't talk a lot about old people. That's because there was little reason to—the command "Honor your father and your mother" pretty much took care of things. And one huge way that people commonly honored their parents was by taking care of them in their old age. When a child grew up, married, and had children, he made sure that his tent or hut or house had enough room for his aging parents, too.

On the other hand, the Bible talks a lot more about the poor, the widows, and the orphans, because *these* were the ones in ancient society who had no one to take care of them, no one to look out for them. These were the ones likely to drift out of community and into isolation—out of contact with everyone else.

Both the Old and New Testaments have clear, specific guidelines about taking care of these people whom society tends to neglect. Today, in our culture, elderly people unfortunately fit that description. Old people (by whatever name you call them: seniors, senior citizens, elders, etc.) are just like us—with the same desires to be included and to talk with people that you have—except that their interactive powers are weakening. They have to work harder to hear a conversation or to get to the mall.

Or even to eat well. That's why organizations like Meals on Wheels exist—to make sure that the physical or emotional health of the elderly isn't compromised by a poor diet.

What can you do, with an organization like Meals on Wheels or by yourself or with your youth group, to make sure that the elderly in your neighborhood, in your church, in your town are well fed?

"Don't throw me aside when I am old; don't desert me when my strength is gone," the psalmist wrote, voicing the fears of many elderly people. We're all following them, you know. Chances are very good that we'll be old someday, too. So treat your older relatives the way you want to be treated when you're their age. Talk. Write. E-mail. Visit.

And feed them.

God Loves Aliens

> Do not exploit the foreigners who live in your
> land. They should be treated like everyone else,
> and you must love them as you love yourself.
> Remember that you were once foreigners in the land
> of Egypt.

Leviticus 19:33-34

If the word alien sounded eerie before 9/11, now it sounds dark and insidious. And thanks to the sensationalism with which most TV networks package their news, a lot of people hear *alien* and think *terrorist*.

Alien, foreigner, traveler, sojourner, pilgrim, immigrant—persons who aren't at home, people who bed down on the road, in a tent, at a motel, in a month-to-month rental. Some aliens want to make their adopted land their home, but the natives can make it hard for them. ("They're not like us . . . can we trust them?") Aliens are typically an underclass in their new country—in a new and very different culture, often surrounded by affluence, isolated by language. Travel to Kuwait City, Los Angeles, Frankfurt, Johannesburg, Chicago, or Bangkok, and you can see entire communities of aliens and immigrants, with languages and habits that strike the natives as exotic, weird, or suspicious.

From the Leviticus verses above, you get an idea of the care that Jews were to give foreigners—after all, the Jews themselves spent a few centuries as aliens in Egypt.

Ironically, in fact, the Jews have spent *most* of their ethnic existence as foreigners—in Egypt, Babylon, Europe—anyplace but the Promised Land. The ancient kingdoms of Israel and Judah didn't survive all that long, and it was only fiftysome years ago that Jews from around the world gathered in Palestine to create the modern nation of Israel.

Gentiles, too, you could say, started out as aliens in the Christian church. The first believers in Jesus, remember, were Jewish, and those Jewish leaders of the early church weren't sure that non-Jews could even qualify as Christians. It took St. Paul to convince them otherwise, thank goodness.

- Do you know any stories of ancestors of yours who were immigrants? If you don't, ask a parent or grandparent, an uncle or aunt for stories. With what ease or difficulty did your foreign ancestor adjust to his or her new country?

- Or are *you* an immigrant? How has it affected the way you treat others?

- Who are the aliens or foreigners at your school or among your neighbors? How are they treated? Why?

Christian Feasting 101: How to Start Feeding People

> Whatever you eat or drink or whatever you do, you must do all for the glory of God.
>
> 1 Corinthians 10:31

In big dinners among many people—that is, what used to be called *feasts*—food, faith, and community intermingle. Feasts for crowds as well as quiet meals for two—we've known all along that when you get at least two people around food, there's more happening than just the physical digestive process. "Breaking bread" has always been naturally associated with deep connections among those at the table.

Ancient Judaism celebrated frequent feasts, and Jesus seems to have been a good Jew in that regard as in others. You'll need both hands and probably a foot or two to count the teaching moments or miracles that were done at meals or feasts recorded in the Bible:

- His first miracle, water changed to wine, he did at a marriage feast.
- On at least two occasions Jesus stretched a few handfuls of bread and fish to feed probably ten-thousand-plus hungry people.

- By eating meals in the homes of "sinners" (like Matthew and Zacchaeus), Jesus illustrated to the Jewish religious leaders how spiritually uppity and just plain wrong they were, and how much better spiritual company the "sinners" made.

- Jesus held a "last supper" before his crucifixion with his disciples. That's at least what Christians traditionally call it—it was really the seder, an old Jewish feast more than a millennium old that was prepared and served during Passover (and which early Christians morphed into "love feasts" of shared meals any old time).

And even today all it takes is a potluck of tuna casseroles or Chinese chicken salad or homemade guacamole and chips to bring people together to feed not only their bodies, but their souls too—to feed on the pleasure of being with and eating with friends, and of connecting socially and emotionally and spiritually.

So designate Fridays as Feast Nite! Everyone bring part of the meal, and share it with good friends from church, from the neighborhood—and also with those you *want* to get to know better. Keep shared meals simple—tacos, spaghetti, and such. If it's summer, fire up the barbecue, and have everyone bring their own meat or veggies to grill. If it's winter, make soup and have everybody bring some of their favorite bread.

If you don't know the pleasure of feeding your friends, you probably won't be motivated to feed strangers—and *those* are the ones that Jesus wants us to take care of.

What Is Your Duty
to the Poor and Hungry?

What Is Your Duty
to the Poor and Hungry?

> Jesus went over to the collection box in the
> Temple and sat and watched as the crowds dropped
> in their money. Many rich people put in large
> amounts. Then a poor widow came and dropped in
> two pennies. He called his disciples to him and
> said, "I assure you, this poor widow has given
> more than all the others have given. For they gave
> a tiny part of their surplus, but she, poor as she
> is, has given everything she has."
>
> Mark 12:41–44

So there you are with your friend, chatting in the church lobby
a few minutes before services begin. You hear it before you
see it—the clattering turns your head and draws your eyes to
the wooden money box for offerings there in the lobby, and
to the obviously affluent woman who had apparently just
dropped a heavy fistful of coins in, her hand still lingering over
the box. You wonder if she lingers in order to be seen. You
(and most everyone in the parking lot) certainly saw her
emerge from her Beemer Z4. She does a hair flip with her
hand, then heads for the sanctuary, her high heels tapping
authoritatively, fashionably across the tiled lobby floor.

Next in line to the collection box is a woman who is obviously several rungs down the socioeconomic ladder. Her only Sabbath finery is a threadbare cardigan, and she wears well-worn dollar-store sneakers. You can't see what she drops into the box, but judging from the slight tinkling her offering makes, it was small. Maybe two coins.

"Well, would you look at that," says a voice behind you. You turn, it's Jesus. He also is watching the scene at the offering box. Then he turns his head to you and looks you in the eye. "So who do you think gave more?"

You tell him that everyone knows Melanie's donations all but built the church gym. What are a couple quarters from this unknown visitor compared to that?

"Hmmm," Jesus says. "Things are not always as they seem. Bless Melanie's heart, but actually, you know, the visitor gave more.

"That visitor lives in government-subsidized housing, stands in line for free cheese and butter at the community center, and works two minimum-wage jobs with no benefits. After rent, utilities, food, and bus fare, fifty cents is just about her total disposable income for the week. And she gave it all here."

So how much do you give? Or let's put it how Jesus calculated it: not *how much* do you give, but *what proportion* of what you have do you give to the poor, the hungry, the homeless?

Listen Up, Class—
This Is Life-and-Death Stuff

Listen Up, Class
This Is Life-and-Death Stuff

> They are gaunt with hunger and flee to the deserts
> and the wastelands, desolate and gloomy. They eat
> coarse leaves, and they burn the roots of shrubs
> for heat.

Job 30:3–4

WHAT IS HUNGER?

It's more than what you see on TV specials about Ethiopia or India. That's only the tip of the iceberg. In fact, there are three broad levels of hunger:

- **Immediate life-threatening hunger** is usually caused by war or famine. This level of hunger has obvious and physically-visible effects—and represents only a fraction of world hunger.

- **Chronic malnourishment** causes one's body to suffer deficiency in calories or other major nutrients most of the time. It results in major health problems, reduced energy levels and work output, and limited life span. This level of hunger affects 700 million people in the world—that's one in eight—and is the cause of high mortality in children.

85

- **Cyclic malnourishment** causes one's body to suffer deficiency in calories *some* of the time—usually seasonally or monthly. This is typical of hunger among those in North America. Cyclic malnourishment results in health problems and reduced energy and work output; and it may over time shorten one's life span. Children suffering this level of hunger are very likely to fall behind in school, which has a major impact on their future.

CONSEQUENCES OF HUNGER

Even if a person is not in danger of imminent starvation, malnourishment impairs one's ability to function in society:

- The reduced work effort caused by chronic hunger disrupts one's family life and economic prospects.
- The threat of disease increases—especially anemia and vitamin-A blindness.
- Child development is impaired—not just stunted physical growth that is visible, but impaired development of the brain, too.
- One in ten chronically hungry children die before their first birthday. That's a global rate of 35,000 per day.

This material is adapted from "Mini-Course on Hunger" on the Web site of Oregon Bread for the World (*http://home.teleport.com/~breador/*)

Give to Those Who Ask. Period.

Give to Those Who Ask. Period.

> Give to those who ask, and don't turn away from
> those who want to borrow.

Matthew 5:42

Beggars have always been with us. You can't help but wonder about something, though: If Christians did their job, would society have fewer beggars?

First, there have always been people who shun domesticity, who flee from social obligations, who are content to live under a bridge, take their meals at the Rescue Mission, bum cigarettes from passersby, and smoke the afternoon away with like-minded friends until the dark or the cold drives them to a makeshift shelter.

Then there are the mentally ill, the chronically irresponsible, the addicts—individuals who would get a job if they could, but they can't. Or they can't keep a job. These are often indistinguishable from the first group.

A third group of beggars don't beg in the traditional sense, but they're still the most traditional. These are the ones who have lost their means of earning a living. They have lost a leg, an arm, or their eyes . . . they have lost their breadwinner or protector . . . they have lost a respectable place in society. They are the lepers of the ancient world, the crippled of the Middle Ages, the optionless of the modern world.

That's right, those with no options. Even in North America, even in Europe—where McDonald's and Starbucks proliferate—there are millions without options. They are poor and undereducated. They go from minimum-wage job to minimum-wage job (often two of these at a time) that offer no benefits, no health insurance, no sick days, no flexibility when it comes to a child's school program or jury duty. They do not live like this because they want to, but because they have no way out. A minor medical emergency or a brake job on their fifteen-year-old car puts them back for months. They have no credit, so they don't go in debt—they just cut back on food, on clothes, on medications. They skip utility payments for a month and hope the gas and electric company doesn't turn off their lights and heat.

One could say that *these* are the modern beggars. They're not out there begging in the streets, but their economic and social situation is identical to traditional beggars.

How do you give to these kinds of beggars?

If you find some of these modern "beggars" and give to them, does it matter how they use the money? If Jesus says to give to those who ask, does it even matter how they use your gift?

Where does common sense enter the picture? Does common sense blunt radical Christian obedience, or does it sharpen it?

Buy Low, Sell High, Share All

Buy Low, Sell High, Share All

> All the believers met together constantly and
> shared everything they had. They sold their
> possessions and shared the proceeds with those in
> need. They worshiped together at the Temple each
> day, met in homes for the Lord's Supper, and
> shared their meals with great joy and generosity—
> all the while praising God and enjoying the
> goodwill of all the people. And each day the Lord
> added to their group those who were being saved.
>
> Acts 2:44–47

You want radical Christian living? Extreme obedience to Jesus? You want to follow the example of the New Testament church? Look no further—it begins right here, at the tail end of Acts 2.

These verses absolutely corner you. There's not even the excuse of, "Well, it depends on how you interpret it" because these verses are so straightforward, so in-your-face, that you can't avoid the plain sense of them. There's no escaping it: Luke wrote that believers in the earliest Christian church sold their possessions then shared the cash they got with those in need. Shared their meals, too, probably with any who wanted to sit down with them, with any who were hungry.

Talk about community! No private property. Everything shared on the basis of need, not desire. Monastic communities have probably been the most visibly and consistently successful at living seriously in community, and for centuries at that.

It is curious that, in the face of this robust and unambiguous example from Christianity's earliest days, "Christian" North America has virtually adopted the very opposite economic model—private ownership of property, free enterprise, and capitalism—often with religious zeal.

The point is, following this relatively untaught New Testament example of sharing everything means you'll be swimming upstream. Against the current. So how do you do it these days, in your world? Is it even possible? How can a North American teenager who really wants to obey God share everything with other believers around you?

When the Bible says these first Christians sold their possessions, notice that they didn't *give* the proceeds to those in need, but *shared* the proceeds with them. Heaven knows they had to live, too.

What about starting by simply sharing whatever community you have? Share yourself now, even while you're asking God to open up future opportunities to get really radical in your sharing.

Equalization Committee

Equalization Committee

Of course, I don't mean you should give so much
that you suffer from having too little. I only
mean that there should be some equality. Right now
you have plenty and can help them. Then at some
other time they can share with you when you need
it. In this way, everyone's needs will be met. Do
you remember what the Scriptures say about this?
"Those who gathered a lot had nothing left over,
and those who gathered only a little had enough."

2 Corinthians 8:13–15

It can be overwhelming if you are aware of those around you with less than you. A lot less. If they're not in your school, then they certainly are in your town, or at least along its fringes. And then there's the world out there, with way too many of its six billion-plus people in various stages of hunger and starvation.

St. Paul was aiming to calm similar anxieties among the Christians he wrote to in ancient Corinth. What with their own needs, the needs of their neighbors, the dire need of other Christians scattered around the Mediterranean—they were stressing out. We only have so much money to throw at all these worthy causes, they were thinking.

No prob, wrote Paul. God doesn't expect you to spend

yourself into oblivion on other people's needs. All God wants is for there to be some equality. At any given time, some have more than they need, and others have less than they need. Those who have more should share their surplus with those who lack what they need. You needn't give away the store—just your extra. That way, everybody has enough. That's what God wants.

So start modestly. Start where you are, where you can make a difference. Like when you hear that a neighbor has suffered a serious setback—job loss, an accident or illness that cuts significantly into work time. Take up a collection among your neighbors! Here's how you may want to organize it, so that it feels natural, and not like some Jerry Lewis Telethon event:

- Write up or practice a brief explanation of why you're collecting money: "Hi, I'm Derry from down the street. Our neighbor, Valerie Combs, just got home from the hospital and can't work for two or three months. What we'd like to do is collect enough cash to pay three of their mortgage payments for them."

- Create a way to confirm to contributors that their donations will indeed be used *only* for the purpose.

- Now go door to door among your neighbors and collect that cash!

- When it's time for your neighborhood to present the cash gift, you can be as quiet or as celebratory as you all want!

Achieving Cosmic Balance

> Then Moses told them, "Do not keep any of it
> overnight." But, of course, some of them didn't
> listen and kept some of it until morning. By then
> it was full of maggots and had a terrible smell.
> And Moses was very angry with them.
>
> Exodus 16:19–20

"Okay, you have your food," Moses said when God left this
white fluffy stuff all over the ground every morning, perfect
for making pita bread out of. "*Now* will you believe God will
take care of you out here in the desert?"

"But what is this stuff?" the people said.

"I have no more idea than you," said Moses. "If you must
call it something, call it *manna*. Oh, and something else.
Don't pick up more than a day's worth. Don't try to hoard it
just so you won't have to go out each morning and gather it
fresh. It won't last in your tents. It goes bad after one day.
Trust me on this."

And of course some Israelites *didn't* trust Moses on this—
they stored some manna in a jar overnight so, come morning,
they could just reach into the jar instead of having to go to the
trouble of getting dressed, putting on their sandals, and going
out into the morning chill to collect manna for that day.

Sure enough, next morning they awoke to a stench like you wouldn't believe—a reek somewhere between rotting rodent and roadkill skunk. Complete with maggots. They couldn't get it out of the tent fast enough, dumping the putrid mess far away from camp.

In this stinky tale lies a reminder for those of us who dwell not in tents but in a culture of accumulation. We must acquire stuff to get along in our world—food, clothes, shoes, books, CDs—but we don't have to *accumulate* stuff.

In a sentence, *when you buy something new, give away something old.* The old "wax on, wax off" karma of *Karate Kid* can be traced directly to God's sense of balance. Jeans in, cords out. *The Matrix Reloaded—Collector's Edition* in, *The Goonies* out. A pair of lilac-scented candles in, a pair of old throw pillows out.

Drop off your old (but still perfectly good) stuff at Salvation Army, Value Village, Ben Israel Synagogue Thrift Store, or St. Vincent's. Or collect it somewhere where your mother won't mind, persuade your friends to do the same, sell it all at a yard sale and send the money to a local or global agency that feeds the hungry.

The result? A semblance of personal balance—plus people with less than you (less stuff, less food, fewer options) will benefit, too.

Front Porch Surprise

So that evening they went out to the camp of the
Arameans, but no one was there! For the Lord had
caused the whole army of Aram to hear the clatter
of speeding chariots and the galloping of horses
and the sounds of a great army approaching. "The
king of Israel has hired the Hittites and
Egyptians to attack us!" they cried out. So they
panicked and fled into the night, abandoning their
tents, horses, donkeys, and everything else, and
they fled for their lives.

When the lepers arrived at the edge of the
camp, they went into one tent after another,
eating, drinking wine, and carrying out silver and
gold and clothing and hiding it.

2 Kings 7:5–8

There's a famine in the Israeli city of Samaria, aggravated by
a siege by the king of Syria, who is letting no food into the
already famished city. Starvation within Samaria's walls,
enemy soldiers outside them. Samaritans are so desperate
that they're resorting to cannibalism.

Scene change to four lepers, sitting just inside the city's
gate. Begging was bad, since no one had enough for themselves, not to mention for a bunch of leprous beggars missing

fingers or feet or noses. They figure as long as they're gonna die, they might as well take their chances with the invading enemy. Their only chance for food is in the Syrian camp.

So out they go, only to discover the camp deserted. God had removed the Syrian threat from Samaria in a curious way and had essentially plopped a feast down right on Samaria's doorstep.

Feasts on doorsteps. It still happens, though in less spectacular ways. And it needs to happen more, judging from the poor and hungry people in your church or neighborhood, in your city or county. Here's how you can be part of the miracle of feeding hungry people near you:

- Determine who needs meals, who lacks food: a family who has recently lost a member to death or divorce . . . a young couple going through a rough patch . . . a neighbor or acquaintance with no family or no nearby family . . . a family whose sole breadwinner is out of work.

- Depending on how much time you have, how elaborate you want to make this culinary surprise, and the circumstances of the persons you're doing this for, drop off either prepared meals (hot soup, casseroles, roasts, salads) or simply foodstuffs (bread, canned goods, frozen meat, fresh veggies).

- With one hungry family, you may want to do this weekly for a month . . . with another, daily for a week.

Have Another Helping . . .

Have Another Helping

You've read several Bible verses (if not chapters) in the past week or so. So consider this a Bible-reading Sabbath for yourself: You won't read any new Bible passages today, but you have a chance today to reflect, ruminate, consider, mull, and weigh what you've already read.

In fact, there's even space here to write down anything that's been boiling around in your head or your heart for the past few days. So if you're the writing type, write on.

THOUGHTS

What's making sense to you about all this hunger stuff so far?

What's not making sense?

FEELINGS

How does what you've read so far make you feel? Did anything in the Bible or in the readings stop you in your tracks, fry your brain, or otherwise rearrange how you feel about poverty, hunger, the hungry, and what the Bible says about them all?

QUESTIONS

What questions are still spinning in your head? What's still unclear to you? What questions do you wish you could ask *us*?

DECISION

Recall the previous ten or so readings in this book. (Yes, of course it's okay to flip back and review them now. . . . Finished? Good.) What one act or conversation or meeting can you realistically vow to do—or *start* doing—within the next ten days? The only criterion is that your act or conversation or meeting must in some way, if ever so small, begin to make at least one person, or one family, or one neighborhood less hungry.

Eat First, Talk Later

> When God's children are in need, be the one to
> help them out. And get into the habit of inviting
> guests home for dinner or, if they need lodging,
> for the night.
>
> Romans 12:13

Hospitality has always been a social and spiritual virtue—not just in Judaism and Islam and Christianity, but among polytheists and pagans, too. It has always been proper to bring strangers and travelers and the needy in out of the weather, to first tend to their bodily comfort and the needs of their animals, to feed them—*then* you settle back with dessert or espressos or pipes well lit and ask, "Who are you, and where do you come from, and where are you going?"

In Genesis 18, Abraham was surprised by three visitors at his tent. He made sure their thirst was quenched, their dusty feet washed . . . he let them snooze in the shade while Sarah made fresh bread and he butchered, dressed, and roasted a calf . . . and only after the guests had eaten were pleasantries exchanged.

Or take a detour into the ancient Greek saga of Odysseus. Look at the bad guys in the *Odyssey*, and you'll see how important the virtue of hospitality was to Homer and to his culture. The Cyclops was a jerk who deserved to be brutally blinded not because he was a one-eyed freak of nature, but because he violated the ancient virtue of hospitality—he ate his guests, for crying out loud. Meanwhile, back in Ithaca with Penelope (Odysseus's very, very patient wife) her suitors exploited her hospitality, daily feasting on the crops and the beef from her farms. And we all know the bloody end that the suitors met when The Man eventually returned home.

Finally, guess what one of the lowest levels of Dante's hell is? Yup, those who betray guests. No wonder Shakespeare's Macbeth has earned such a despicable place among murderers: It wasn't a common murder he committed—the Scot knifed a guest sleeping under Macbeth's own roof.

St. Paul reminded Roman Christians that they were by no means to let this virtue of hospitality slip out of their own behavior. If pagans were gonna badmouth Christians, it wouldn't be because Christians ignored the hungry, the needy, the strangers in a strange town.

How do you practice hospitality? How do you feed those who are hungry? Does Paul's mandate no longer apply if everyone you know is already well fed? What about those you know *about* who aren't well fed? How can you extend hospitality to the hungry in another city, another country, another continent?

Don't Keep Your Distance

> Share each other's troubles and problems, and in this way obey the law of Christ. If you think you are too important to help someone in need, you are only fooling yourself. You are really a nobody.
>
> Galatians 6:2–3

What exactly are "each other's troubles and problems"? Listen to St. Margaret of Cortona, who wrote this in the thirteenth century:

> I do not want to keep anything that is given to me. I want to experience hunger in order to feed the poor. I want to strip myself in order to clothe them. I want to suffer from need in order to let them enjoy plenty. Prevent people from giving me anything at all, for it is my heart's desire to run to Christ without being weighed down by burdens. (*The Revelations of Margaret of Cortona: The Franciscan Magdalene*)

Okay, so Margaret's idea of carrying the problems of others is a tad on the extreme side for most of us. (Remember, however, she was not married—and as St. Paul reminded us, not that we didn't know it already, living with and loving a spouse just takes a huge bite out of whatever time or energy you have for serving God.) Still, you get the idea: Sharing each other's problems and troubles means living with the same limitations that those others have. At *least* it means living simply.

"You will have found Christ," wrote American novelist Flannery O'Connor in a letter, "when you are concerned with other people's sufferings and not your own."

Like, for example, Margaret of Cortona. When she was seventeen she fled a harsh stepmother (yes, that sort of thing didn't happen just in fairy tales) and moved in with a young nobleman for nine years. He died when she was a mere twenty-six, leaving her with a young son. Her father and stepmom refused to take her back, so she found refuge with the Franciscans, whose order she eventually joined. Besides the prayer and contemplation that all monastics did, Margaret spent the rest of her fifty years serving the poor and the sick—in fact, she founded a hospital and a Franciscan group that looked after the welfare of prisoners and tended their needs.

St. Margaret apparently took Paul's words to the Galatians at face value. She shared the troubles and problems of the poor, the hungry, and the sick with a vengeance—a vengeance against apathy, against seeing misery but not doing anything to relieve it, against thinking herself too important to help someone in need.

- What one person do you know well who has problems that you could share in?

- Honest now: In what ways have you fooled yourself into keeping a safe distance from people in trouble, from people with problems?

That Look in Your Eye

That Look in Your Eye

As they approached the Temple, a man lame from
birth was being carried in. When he saw Peter and
John about to enter, he asked them for some money.

Peter and John looked at him intently, and
Peter said, "Look at us!" The lame man looked at
them eagerly, expecting a gift. But Peter said, "I
don't have any money for you. But I'll give you
what I have. In the name of Jesus Christ of
Nazareth, get up and walk!"

Acts 3:2–6

Works of mercy are about establishing
relationships. It is through the movement of grace
on relationships between persons that wonderful,
even miraculous, things happen.

Robert Smith, S.F.O., personal letter,

in *When Did I See You Hungry?*

by G. T. Straub

You get the idea that when Jesus did miracles for people—or
Peter, or Paul, or any of the Old Testament prophets, for
that matter—they looked the person in the eye. A meal
was usually involved, whether before or after the miracle.
None of these miracle workers wrote out miracle checks of

some sort, then called and left the message, "Your miracle is in the mail."

This is why child-welfare agencies and organizations that feed the hungry connect donors with specific children as much as possible. If you donate regularly, you're sent a photo of the child you're supporting. You're not just mailing a check for $25 or $30 to an organization—the ideal is, you're forging a relationship (albeit not a face-to-face one) with a boy in Ecuador, a girl in Malawi, a teenager in Pakistan. The organization often facilitates letter writing between the two of you.

Chances are, it is the power of a relationship that fuels any works of mercy that you do. A mission trip with your youth group to Mexico. Volunteering in a soup kitchen that feeds downtown transients. Cleaning rooms for a weekend in temporary housing for homeless mothers and their children. You see these individuals, you smell their circumstances, you understand how few if any options they have—and all of a sudden you are moved a bit more than you were before to do works of mercy for them.

Acts of grace and miracles tend to occur most often in relationships. What relationships are you forming with people that need grace and miracles? Should you step outside of your normal, comfortable circle of friends and begin cultivating relationships with people *unlike* yourself? What would that look like?

I'm a Biblical Christian—I Do What the Bible Says (I Think . . .)

> Stop oppressing those who work for you. Treat them fairly and give them what they earn. I want you to share your food with the hungry and to welcome poor wanderers into your homes. . . . If you do these things, your salvation will come like the dawn.
>
> Isaiah 58:6–8

> Solitude and silence may be the meat and potatoes of our prayer lives, but they are empty of nourishment when separated from service of our brothers and sisters.
>
> John Kirvan, *God Hunger*

Oh, how we pick and choose the kind of spirituality we want. We say we're "people of the Book," or that all we want is to obey the Bible, or that we desire authentic worship, or that all we want is to be sold out 100 percent to God (now what *does* that look like, anyway?).

Yet have you ever wondered about why you or your church practices the sacraments or ordinances it does? Take baptism, for instance—an almost universally practiced sacrament in Christianity. Many people interpret Matthew 28:19

105

as a command to baptize, but what about other commands, like foot washing? Should we argue that other commands are "ambiguous" just because they are less common practices or we don't feel as comfortable with them?

The point is, we're human. We pray in ways that are familiar to us. When silence or solitude or candles become (again) spiritually hip, we will do that. We interpret the Bible according to what we already believe, so that verses about foot washing or about women covering their heads when they pray don't really apply to us.

So what do we do with the straight-up words of our Lord when he said through the prophet Isaiah, "Stop oppressing those who work for you. Treat them fairly and give them what they earn. I want you to share your food with the hungry and to welcome poor wanderers into your homes. . . . If you do these things, your salvation will come like the dawn" (58:6–8)?

Does God really mean it? Is there any reason *not* to interpret these words of God literally? Are we uncomfortable with the idea that feeding people and bringing the poor into our homes is tightly linked with our salvation? If we are uncomfortable with it, should we get over it or do something about it? Or does it even matter to God?

Say or Do?

"I can't see your faith if you don't have good deeds, but I will show you my faith through my good deeds."

Do you still think it's enough just to believe that there is one God? Well, even the demons believe this, and they tremble in terror! Fool! When will you ever learn that faith that does not result in good deeds is useless?

Don't you remember that our ancestor Abraham was declared right with God because of what he did when he offered his son Isaac on the altar? You see, he was trusting God so much that he was willing to do whatever God told him to do. His faith was made complete by what he did—by his actions.

James 2:18-22

Love itself is related more to what we do than what we say.

(St. Ignatius of Loyola, *The Spiritual Exercises of St. Ignatius*)

Ignatius (ig-NAY-shus) was born Inigo Lopez de Loyola in Spain. He grew up among nobility, acquiring a taste for rich food, good wine, and fast women. Wounded in battle, he took a long time to convalesce. Though he longed for romance

novels during his recuperation, it is said, all there was to read
was the life of Christ and of the saints. So he read that instead.
And the eventual result of that limited reading matter was
Loyola's founding of the Jesuits—an order of Roman Catholic
priests that specialize not only in evangelism and education, but
also in the cultivation and teaching of spiritual exercises and the
advocacy for all who are socially marginalized: the poor, immigrants, refugees, and underserved minorities, among others.
Jesuits are lawyers, professors, prison chaplains, and missionaries. According to their Web site (jesuit.org), they are called to
"work with and for those people whose needs arise from their
social marginalization."

The spirit of Ignatius and the Jesuits is the same spirit that
blessed the family of five that had just moved into the impossi-
bly small and dilapidated house known to locals as "the Sverik
place"—five acres that had been homesteaded decades ago by
an immigrant family of that name, but that had been vacant for
several years now. The house—more of a hunter's cabin,
really—needed a lot of work, which of course the new owners
couldn't afford. This was rural America, the economy was
dropping off, and the first to suffer from rising interest rates
was the lumber industry: Plywood plants, the big employers in
the area, were laying off people right and left.

One day not long after they moved in, the family got a call
from the elderly pastor of a church just down the road where
they had begun attending. "I hear your place needs some
fixin' up," he said. "We'll be over Saturday morning to help.
We'll even bring the donuts."

Sure enough, Saturday morning saw eight or ten men descend on the house with their tool belts and power tools. They replaced a rotten wall, firmed up the posts in the dirt basement that supported the floor, tore out the bad bathroom plumbing, and sweated together new copper lines to the sink and tub.

The elderly pastor was there, too, doing what he could to run errands and nail the occasional sheetrock nail. During a break in the work, he found himself standing next to the family's husband. "We do this sort of thing now and then," he confided in the young man. "A couple of months ago a bunch of us put a new roof on the Sherman barn, over toward Union Mills, after a fire burned it off. Unlike you, he hadn't come to our church for years. Didn't matter. We built an entire roof—rafters, plywood, shingles, everything—in a day. Didn't invite him to church, either—it would have ruined it."

The apostle James and Ignatius, among others, had it right: Love that you *do* is usually a whole lot more authentic than love you *say*.

Just the Hunger Facts, Ma'am

Just the Hunger Facts, Ma'am

> A hungry person dreams of eating but is still hungry. A thirsty person dreams of drinking but is still faint from thirst when morning comes.
>
> Isaiah 29:8

WHO AND HOW MANY ARE HUNGRY?
Internationally:

- The largest number of hungry people live in South Asia.

- The area with the highest ratio of hungry people is Africa.

In the U.S.:

- One in eight persons are poor (that's 37 million) and, generally, cyclically hungry.
- One in five children are poor.
- Children have the highest poverty rate of any age group.
- The U.S. has the highest child poverty rate of any developed country.

Hunger is actually decreasing . . .

Worldwide, it has decreased over the last three decades, according to United Nations estimates:

- In 1970, 918 million people worldwide (35 percent of the world) were hungry.
- In 1992, 841 million people (20 percent) were hungry.

Progress has been made. World hunger *can* be alleviated. Yet there's still a lot to do. Hunger is a basic need that, when unsatisfied, blocks out all other pursuits. A life spent chronically or cyclically malnourished is a life of limited opportunities, illness, and often premature death.

WHAT CAUSES HUNGER?
What the typical cause of hunger *isn't*:

- A shortage of food
- Too many people
- Lazy people

What the typical cause of hunger *is*:

An inability to grow or earn enough income to buy sufficient food and secure other vital needs—like shelter, health care.

In short, the cause of hunger is *poverty*.

Enough food is grown worldwide. The problem is that

many people can't produce or buy all they need. They must have a) land or b) an income.

Earning a sufficient income requires three things:

- *Sufficient opportunities*, like a plentiful enough supply of jobs and entrepreneurial investment.
- *Skills* to match the available opportunities. This means training and education must be available.
- *A political and social environment* that is free from discrimination, corruption, and war, so that people can freely develop their skills and pursue opportunities.

THE END OF CLASS QUIZ (Please use a sharpened #2 pencil.)

1. Any fact here surprise you? Like maybe the one about there's really no shortage of food in the world? Or that world hunger has actually *decreased* in the past thirty years?

2. Do you really think you'd recognize the hungry poor in the U.S. if you saw them? What could you do to help feed them?

This material is adapted from "Mini-Course on Hunger" on the Web site of Oregon Bread for the World (*http://home.teleport.com/~breador/*).

A Follower of Brother Porsche

As Jesus was going down the road, he saw Matthew
sitting at his tax-collection booth. "Come, be my
disciple," Jesus said to him. So Matthew got up
and followed him.

That night Matthew invited Jesus and his
disciples to be his dinner guests, along with his
fellow tax collectors and many other notorious
sinners. The Pharisees were indignant. "Why does
your teacher eat with such scum?" they asked his
disciples.

When he heard this, Jesus replied, "Healthy
people don't need a doctor—sick people do." Then he
added, "Now go and learn the meaning of this
Scripture: 'I want you to be merciful; I don't want
your sacrifices.' For I have come to call sinners,
not those who think they are already good enough."

Matthew 9:9–13

First-century tax collectors were financially ambitious. They
had to be. They were the financial planners and stockbrokers
of their day. If they didn't belong to the top quarter or so of
society, they were headed in that direction. They might be
driving a nice but preowned Subaru now, but they had their
sights set on Mercedes, Expeditions, and Beemers.

Matthew the tax collector wasn't looking for a messiah—he was looking for more shekels, for a larger commission, for a bigger cut of the Judeans' tax payments that the Roman government authorized him to receive.

This kind we will always have with us. Fast forward a couple millennia to TV producer and author Gerard Thomas Straub, who "chased after Brother Porsche," he says, long before he discovered St. Francis of Assisi and wrote a book about him.

Okay, we'll take it slow for you:

Matthew: became a disciple of Jesus.

Gerard Thomas Straub: a television producer for popular soap operas ("General Hospital" and "The Doctors"). Raised as a Catholic, he fell into a bout of atheism after a disillusioning stint working for televangelist Pat Robertson's Christian Broadcasting Network, and the *700 Club* in particular. Still, blessed with a seeker's soul and a novelist's imagination, he couldn't stay away from the quest for spiritual understanding, which led him to explore the life of Francis of Assisi.

Francis of Assisi: the founder of the Franciscan monastic order and fervent advocate of a life of poverty among the poor as the only authentic way to God. You know, the rich twelfth-century Italian brat whom God finally got a hold of, who alienated his affluent and respectable father by selling his horse and armor and giving the money to a chapel in disrepair. Finally, when Francis's father took his own son to court in order to legally withdraw his inheritance from him, Francis stood before the bishop, removed all his clothes (yup, we mean *all*), and by this act symbolized his total surrender of all worldly goods, honors, and privileges. Then, naked to the world, he walked out of court and into the hills, eventually to found the Franciscan order of monks, known for their poverty, their community, and their acts of love and help to those who need them.

So this was the medieval man who fascinated the twentieth-century Straub, and who opened that media man's eyes to the poor, the hungry, and the homeless. He consequently picked up a camera and set off for the armpits of the world—the slums of Calcutta and Manila, the tenements of Los Angeles, the shanties of Kingston, Jamaica. The result was a photo-essay of "the least of these." The *real* result was a broken heart and completely new priorities for Straub.

Brother Francis or Brother Porsche—which one is being followed by those you know? By you?

This Do in Remembrance of Me— and of the Hungry Everywhere

This Do in Remembrance of Me and of the Hungry Everywhere

As they were eating, Jesus took a loaf of bread and asked God's blessing on it. Then he broke it in pieces and gave it to the disciples, saying, "Take it, for this is my body."

And he took a cup of wine and gave thanks to God for it. He gave it to them, and they all drank from it. And he said to them, "This is my blood, poured out for many, sealing the covenant between God and his people."

Mark 14:22–24

Sometime in your life, hope that you might see one starved man, the look on his face when the bread finally arrives. Hope that you might have baked it or bought it or even kneaded it yourself. For that look on his face, for your eyes meeting his eyes across a piece of bread, you might be willing to lose a lot, or suffer a lot, or die a little even.

Daniel Berrigan, S.J., from an address given at
the College of Wooster, February 1991

Communion, the Lord's Supper, Eucharist, Love Feast. Bread and wine. The fundamental staples of physical life. Well, in

116

Jesus' culture, at least. If Jesus had come to twentieth-century Bozeman or Boston instead of to first-century Judea, who knows but that it might have been a hamburger and a Coke, or tofu and raw juice, or bagel and coffee.

That "last supper" Jesus had with his disciples was actually a seder meal and the ritual cups of wine and the bread had their own Jewish symbolism, reminding all at the table of how God delivered his people from the misery of Egyptian slavery. The Cup of Remembrance, for instance— which Jesus was probably drinking when he said, "Drink this in remembrance of *me*." And the flat bread—a reminder not only of how hurriedly they left Egypt (no time for bread to rise, just a yeastless bread), but of the miraculous, bread-like manna that God provided for them in the desert.

What else can communion remind us of, as we sit there staring at the thin wafer between thumb and finger, at the plastic thimble of grape juice? Maybe how most of the world lacks adequate food and drink? Could the bread and wine of Eucharist also remind us of how part of following Christ's example is feeding others physically as Christ feeds us symbolically at communion?

No Islands in This Sea of Humanity

No Islands in This Sea of Humanity

> If one part suffers, all the parts suffer with it,
> and if one part is honored, all the parts are glad.
> Now all of you together are Christ's body, and
> each one of you is a separate and necessary part
> of it.
>
> 1 Corinthians 12:26–27

"No man is an island, entire of itself," wrote the seventeenth-century poet-theologian John Donne. "Every man is a piece of the continent, a part of the main. . . . Any man's death diminishes me, because I am involved in mankind; and therefore never send to know for whom the bell tolls; it tolls for thee."

Then nearly four centuries later, along came Henri Nouwen—an insecure priest, academic, and author of books on spirituality. He lived his last decade near Toronto at L'Arche Daybreak, where he was the pastor in this Christian home for people with developmental disabilities. It was at L'Arche where he discovered what it meant to *be* rather than to *do:*

> What we desire most is to do away with suffering by fleeing from it or finding a quick cure for it. We want to earn our bread by making a real contribution. This means first and foremost doing something to show that our presence makes

118

a difference. And so we ignore our greatest gift, which is our ability to enter into solidarity with those who suffer. (*The Way of the Heart: Desert Spirituality and Contemporary Ministry*)

Did you catch that? Our greatest gift is to "enter into solidarity with those who suffer." And what exactly does that mean?

Probably something like what St. Paul wrote to the Christians in ancient Corinth, and what John Donne preached to his congregation of English men and women in 1624: Solidarity begins with seeing the interconnectedness of you with others.

Fulfilling our obligation to others, Nouwen suggests, is not *doing* so much as *being:* "Our presence makes a difference." Our *greatest* gift can be simply (but profoundly) entering into the suffering of the poor and hungry.

Okay, you're probably not in a position to do this. You're in school, you live at home, your life is still not wholly your own in some important ways. But you see why the saints were called saints—you see the ideal they came close to achieving, an ideal you would do well to strive for even though you might not realistically reach it in the near future.

Besides, as you get older, you'll find yourself entering into the suffering of a lot of people, in ways you can't anticipate.

Small Things

> . . . good deeds, such as bringing up children,
> showing hospitality, washing the feet of God's
> people, helping those in trouble . . .
>
> 1 Timothy 5:10, NIV

> Even if you write a letter for a blind man, or
> you just sit and listen to someone, or you take
> the mail for him, or you visit somebody or bring a
> flower to somebody, or wash clothes for somebody
> or clean the house—small things, but God sees
> everything great.
>
> Mother Teresa, *The Joy in Loving*

The small things we do for each other—are they really so small? Maybe under the surface, just out of our sight, some of them are big things. Maybe one or two of them are huge things.

If you've read Harper Lee's *To Kill a Mockingbird*, you remember when old, ugly, rude Mrs. Dubose asked the boy Jem to come read to her every afternoon after school. His heart sank at this assignment, but his father Atticus gave him no choice but to accept the horrid request.

Jem showed up on Mrs. Dubose's front porch with fear and trembling that first afternoon, and twenty minutes into *Ivanhoe* it became clear that Mrs. Dubose wasn't listening.

Jem looked up from the book to where she lay in bed—her head was back, her mouth open and drooling a little, as if a subtle, silent fit was upon her. The alarm rang and the hired girl swept into the room, shooing the children out. "Time for her medicine," she said.

The reading assignment soon became a habit—no longer scary, just tedious now. And Jem discovered a pattern: Each day he had been staying a little longer at Mrs. Dubose's, her alarm clock went off a few minutes later each day, and she was into one of her fits when it went off.

She died only a couple months later, and only then did Atticus tell Jem that Mrs. Dubose had been addicted to morphine, having been given it by a doctor years earlier as a pain killer. But she was determined, she had confided to Atticus, "to leave this world beholden to nothing and nobody" when she died. And Jem's reading was the distraction that Mrs. Dubose needed to gradually extend the time between her morphine doses, until she didn't need them at all.

To Jem, it was a boring hour or two for a month. But he didn't know the half of it. This was a Big Thing to Mrs. Dubose.

Somehow, there are no small things to God. They're all big things. Give what you can give and do what you can do—and let God make your small part a big thing to an Asian or African child you will never meet, but who will live a little longer, be a little healthier, have a bit more hope—a Big Thing—because of your small thing.

Have Another Helping . . .

Have Another Helping . . .

Y ou've read several Bible verses (if not chapters) in the past week or so. So consider this a Bible-reading Sabbath for yourself: You won't read any new Bible passages today, but you have a chance today to reflect, ruminate, consider, mull, and weigh what you've already read.

In fact, there's even space here to write down anything that's been boiling around in your head or your heart for the past few days. So if you're the writing type, write on.

THOUGHTS

What's making sense to you about all this hunger stuff so far?

What's not making sense?

FEELINGS

How does what you've read so far make you feel? Did anything in the Bible or in the readings stop you in your tracks, fry your brain, or otherwise rearrange how you feel about poverty, hunger, the hungry, and what the Bible says about them all?

QUESTIONS

What questions are still spinning in your head? What's still unclear to you? What questions do you wish you could ask *us*?

DECISION

Recall the previous ten or so readings in this book. (Yes, of course it's okay to flip back and review them now. . . . Finished? Good.) What one act or conversation or meeting can you realistically vow to do—or *start* doing—within the next ten days? The only criterion is that your act or conversation or meeting must in some way, if ever so small, begin to make at least one person or one family or one neighborhood less hungry.

Each of Us . . . Just a Little

> Then the LORD turned to him and said, "Go with
> the strength you have and rescue Israel from the
> Midianites. I am sending you!"
>
> "But Lord," Gideon replied, "how can I rescue
> Israel? My clan is the weakest in the whole
> tribe of Manasseh, and I am the least in my
> entire family!"
>
> Judges 6:14–15

It wasn't even a kingdom yet—just several hundred thousand squatters, really, whose one-and-only God Yahweh told them that this was their land, in spite of the pagan occupants already there.

Add to that the situation at the time: The marauding Midianites had beaten down the Israelites, stripping their crops bare and rustling their livestock. Their vegetable gardens in ruins, their barley fields trampled, their meat stolen— Israel was looking at slow starvation.

In the nick of time, God tapped Gideon—the youngest of his family, his clan Israel's weakest. It was like your high school's athletic director looking for a quarterback and choosing a 115-pound freshman whose idea of fun was two hours after school every day in the computer lab. That or chess club.

Gideon, of course, had the good sense to object. He was a nobody, he claimed. He was fearful, threshing wheat at a *winepress*, of all places, to keep out of sight of the occupying army of Midianites. And he was skeptical, requiring several signs from God that God indeed meant what he said.

A nobody. Fearful. Skeptical. Were these mere alibis? Was Gideon trying to squirrel out of something? Or did he really think himself unfit for the job?

Didn't matter, God said. You, Gideon, freshman nerd though you may be (or may not)—you're the one to lead the varsity to victory this weekend.

Now consider yourself. Why would anyone think *you* could make a difference in the world? A difference, say, in whether a child in Gabon eats or dies of starvation.

What possible difference can *you* make in such dire circumstances? You may feel a lot like Gideon: fearful of giving money that, frankly, you really can't afford to give. Skeptical about what good would come, anyway, from the little you can contribute to a cause.

Okay, you're right about one thing—there are no guarantees. Yet in some ways, there's a big fat guarantee, and this is it: When you do good for someone else, it's never wasted. You may not see the effects of your action (because you're not near to see it or because the effects don't materialize until long after you're gone), or the effects of your good intentions may not be what you expected—but that doesn't mean there weren't any.

Why You Give What You Give

Whatever you eat or drink or whatever you do, you must do all for the glory of God.

1 Corinthians 10:31

It is not how much you give, but with how much love you give it.

Mother Teresa

Virtue itself turns vice, being misapplied,
And vice sometime's by action dignified.

William Shakespeare, *Romeo and Juliet*

Let us talk about motives. Why do you do the good you do?

For starters, does it even matter? The older you get, the more you'll become aware of how very good things are done by very questionable people. Andrew Carnegie chewed up and spit out thousands upon thousands of men and their families in his steel mills—paid them as little as he could, made them dependent on those poverty wages, and put them out on the streets when they were no longer useful to him. Yet late in his life, in a spasm of conscience, he donated many millions of his obscenely extravagant earnings to build and endow libraries (2,800 of 'em), schools,

126

colleges, and other cultural and scientific institutions across the country.

Now, a century later, there is hardly a county in the country that has not benefited somehow from Carnegie's philanthropy. If not locally—as with a city library or school grant—then by Carnegie-endowed institutions that have funded astrophysicists who discovered the expansion of the universe, researchers who proved DNA is the genetic material, and writers who created *Sesame Street*. Much good was done— derived, however, at much human cost.

What were Carnegie's motives behind his deep cultural contributions? Or Newman's? Perhaps no one but Carnegie and Newman themselves will ever know, in Mother Teresa's words, with how much love he gave away his money.

It is curious that few organizations turn away contributions (especially large ones) because of the contributor's motives. Does the contributor want a tax deduction? Need to shine up her public image? Have a heart for the cause he's giving to? As long as the contribution is legal and there is no bad publicity from it, little is said except, "Thank you very much."

God, however, looks at the giver's motives. Which makes the tiny amounts most of us are able to give absolutely huge. Not huge on the ledger, but spiritually, cosmically, somehow huge.

Golden Goblets and Hearing Aids

Soon a Samaritan woman came to draw water, and
Jesus said to her, "Please give me a drink."

John 4:7

Of what use is it to weigh down Christ's table
with golden cups, when he himself is dying of
hunger? First, fill him when he is hungry; then use
the means you have left to adorn his table. Will
you have a golden cup made but not give a cup of
water? What is the use of providing the table with
cloths woven of gold thread, and not providing
Christ himself with the clothes he needs?

St. John Chrysostom, from a homily on the Gospel of Matthew

Not many churches display golden cups and cloths of golden
thread on their communion tables or altars these days. That
was the church of the Middle Ages, right? When church
leaders were powerful political leaders, when the church was
into gaudy shows of luxury—not like today.

Think again. It might not be golden cups or gold-woven
tablecloths, but there are other ways that prosperous
twenty-first-century churches display their wealth. Sound
and light systems that, back in the sixties, the Rolling Stones
would have been jealous of. Pipe organs that rattle the walls

with their volume and resonance. Sanctuaries that are air-conditioned, spacious as a Home Depot, whose pastors have connections with governors, senators, and presidents.

These are our golden cups and golden tablecloths. St. John Chrysostom's words, therefore, are as valid for us as they were to an affluent medieval church. If your church must have the latest sound system, let it first give hearing to an older man in town whose Social Security checks barely let him pay for rent, heat, and food—and who cannot afford a hearing aid. Your church (says John Chrysostom) should first buy him a hearing exam and hearing aid, then invest in its state-of-the-art sound system.

If your church needs a new building for classrooms or offices or worship, let it first do something about affordable housing for the poor in its neighborhood. Maybe your church's parishioners include attorneys who could press the city or landlords for rent control. Or maybe members of your church could add a critically needed bedroom to the small house of a poor, growing family in your neighborhood.

If your church wants a new piano or organ or drum set, let it first donate instruments to a city school that can't afford instruments for its band. Or donate the funds for a part-time music teacher to a school in a low socioeconomic community, whose students wouldn't otherwise be exposed to music.

Give a cup of cold water to someone who really needs it, *then* build the fountain for the church lobby.

Just One, One, One

Just One, One, One

> Because one person disobeyed God, many people
> became sinners. But because one other person
> obeyed God, many people will be made right in
> God's sight.
>
> Romans 5:19

"Bird by bird, buddy. Just take it bird by bird."

Father-to-son advice, given more than three decades ago to a ten-year-old boy overwhelmed and panicked by the hugeness of a science report on birds. That boy's sister—Anne Lamott—overheard and remembered her father's advice, which she also found valuable in her writing career. In fact, those words became the title of her book about (guess what) writing.

"Bird by bird" is good advice for more than science projects and writing. Mother Teresa said the same thing in different words, and not about writing, but about loving people practically:

> I never look at the masses as my responsibility. I look only at the individual. I can love only one person at a time. I can feed only one person at a time.
>
> Just one, one, one . . .
>
> The whole work is only a drop in the ocean. But if we

130

don't put the drop in, the ocean would be one drop less.

Same thing for you. Same thing in your family. Same thing in the church where you go. Just begin . . . one, one, one.*

One by one by one. In a letter to Christians who lived in Rome—the Hong Kong or Manhattan of the ancient world—St. Paul wrote about the significance of one. It took just one man, he explained—that would be Adam—to introduce sin into humanity. By the same token it took just one Man to heal those sin-infected humans.

One man, one step, one person, one act at a time. Results are often long in coming, and even longer before you *see* those results. When you do what is right, especially toward someone else, especially if that someone else is hungrier or colder or sicker or poorer than you—then God makes it all work somehow. It may seem ridiculous to you how your ten bucks a month can actually feed a child, or how much it helps to give one child in Detroit or Djibouti school clothes so she can attend classes without humiliation.

Yet one reason Mother Teresa was, well, Mother Teresa was that she was content dealing with the poor one at a time. She acted according to what she woke up to each morning. A diseased mother on Monday, a United Nations address on Tuesday. It didn't matter. Bird by bird. One, one, one.

What one will you reach out to today? This week? This year?

*Quoted by Andrew Harvey, editor, The Essential Mystics: The Soul's Journey into Truth.

Live Simply

Look at the birds. They don't need to plant or
harvest or put food in barns because your heavenly
Father feeds them. And you are far more valuable
to him than they are. Can all your worries add a
single moment to your life? Of course not.

And why worry about your clothes? Look at the
lilies and how they grow. They don't work or make
their clothing, yet Solomon in all his glory was
not dressed as beautifully as they are. And if God
cares so wonderfully for flowers that are here
today and gone tomorrow, won't he more surely care
for you? You have so little faith!

So don't worry about having enough food or
drink or clothing. Why be like the pagans who are
so deeply concerned about these things? Your
heavenly Father already knows all your needs, and
he will give you all you need from day to day if
you live for him and make the Kingdom of God your
primary concern.

So don't worry about tomorrow, for tomorrow
will bring its own worries. Today's trouble is
enough for today.

Matthew 6:26–34

The amount of energy used by one American is
equivalent to that used by 3 Japanese, 14 Chinese,
or 168 Bangladeshi people.

From *Simpler Living, Compassionate Life:*
A Christian Perspective, edited by Michael Schut

Live simply, says the guru.

Buy it big and buy it now, says the global marketing machine.

Look at the birds and the fields, says Jesus, and you'll see a good reason to stop obsessing about rent and groceries and worn-out shoes.

If you *do* slow down long enough to look at the birds and fields and everything else in God's showcase called creation, it will probably occur to you that just maybe you ought to live simpler than you do. For that is at least one lesson lurking behind these words of Jesus: that we worry far too much about some things.

If God cares well for us, then perhaps we should look to those who are hungrier or colder or poorer than us and figure out ways to convert a simpler lifestyle of ours into a more tolerable lifestyle for them. You may need to recruit your household on some of these ideas.

For example, spend the next thirty days cutting the amount of electricity and natural gas you traditionally use—and then donate the difference to an organization that feeds the hungry, whether in your own area or across the ocean. (In most cases you'll not only be feeding the hungry with what you save, but you'll be doing your environment a favor, too.)

- When you do laundry, use a drying rack or a line in your basement or hang your clothes out instead of using a dryer.

- Take short showers. Heating water consumes a *lot* of energy. (You could treat yourself once a week to a long shower.)

- Turn off lamps and stereos before you leave your room or house or apartment. They don't consume as much energy as your fridge, dryer, and hot water heater, but turning off a half dozen lightbulbs that you normally leave burning can save some bucks. While you're at it, swap your incandescent bulbs for florescent lights.

- Check out **energyhawk.com**—or the Web site of your local energy provider—for tips on decreasing the amount of electricity and natural gas you use. Print the chart at **citypublicservice.com/images/conserve_billchart.gif** to track your energy usage month to month.

- If you can, ride your bike or walk instead of driving. *Big* savings here.

Sure, doing any *one* of these things will inconvenience you. But are you willing to inconvenience yourself for a month—or for several months, or for a lifetime—if it means creating money to feed people who would otherwise die from diseases caused by malnutrition if not by outright starvation?

Why Are People Hungry?

A poor person's farm may produce much food, but injustice sweeps it all away.

Proverbs 13:23

There is enough food on this planet to feed its people. All its people. Yet at least 800 million people suffer from hunger, from the kind of chronic malnutrition that eventually kills, or from outright starvation. That's one-sixth of the world's population.

How can there be enough food, yet we still have starving people? Try these stats on for size:

- Percentage of all meat and fish eaten by the richest fifth of the world's people: **45**
- Percentage of all meat and fish eaten by the poorest fifth of the world's people: **5**
- Percentage of all malnourished children who live in countries with food surpluses: **80***

Then why do so many people go hungry?

Over and over again in the research, you read that lack of food is not the reason for hunger, malnourishment, or under-nourishment. The main reason is lack of money to buy food. Poverty.

What then should be our response toward the poor? What are our options if lack of money is why people are hungry? The options that leap to mind are to give poor people money, give poor people jobs, or change the system that keeps the poor poor.

You can now see that when you define the problem of hunger this way, you're walking into a minefield of ideologies and politics. Do we merely give away money to people who claim to be poor? How do we know if they're really poor? What if they're just lazy and want a handout from the government, a church, or a charitable organization? Is it worth giving money to supposedly undeserving people if truly deserving people are helped in the process?

Or should we give poor people jobs instead of cash? The president of your grandparents or great-grandparents, Franklin Delano Roosevelt, is famous (infamous, to some people) for creating jobs simply in order to put American men back to work during the Great Depression of the 1930s. The government concocted building projects for unemployed men to work on, just so those men could be paid for their work and could then put a roof over the heads of their families. And feed them.

Or should we change the system that keeps poor people poor? This is a particularly dicey option. In *Sister Earth: Creation, Ecology, and the Spirit*, Dom Helder Camara writes, "When I give food to the poor, they call me a saint. When I asked why the poor have no food, they call me a communist." Our current global financial system is responsible for much that is good and much that is bad. Kind of like life. The trick is changing the system so that it no longer rewards the powerful at the expense of the powerless, yet without losing what the system does well.

Good luck. Not impossible, but immensely difficult.

You may be one that will someday have the vision and influence to make such changes for the sake of the world's poor and hungry. Meanwhile, you're like the rest of us— taking care of your neighbor, wherever you are, especially if your neighbor is hungrier or colder or poorer than you. That at least Jesus made plain to us.

*From itdg.org, the Web site of ITDG (Intermediate Technology Development Group).

10 Minutes a Day . . .

> Fool! When will you ever learn that faith that
> does not result in good deeds is useless?
>
> James 2:20

If you were to spend just ten minutes a day thinking about how you can prudently do something for the hungry in your neighborhood and in the world, here are some starting places:

Register the hungry poor to vote.

Why? Although only 60 percent of all Americans voted in the 2000 election, 86 percent of *all registered voters* turned out to vote. Moral? When people are registered, they vote.

There's more: thirty percent of the American voting-age public is *un*registered. That's nearly 63 million unregistered American citizens of voting age (eighteen and older). And guess who are a huge slice of these 63 million? Poor people. Hungry people. Moms and dads who can't get off work to vote, who don't have a car, or who can't get to the polling place.

Yet the poor have real influence, if only it can be bent toward the voting booth. Remember the 85 million unregistered Americans of voting age? You had better believe they'd have the influence of a T-Rex if they actually voted. Here's how you can help them do just that. Get in touch with existing voter-registration efforts of your state or county, or with political candidates who are mounting registration drives.

Get your youth group involved in feeding the hungry.

- Contact local programs to see what their needs are—organizations like Meals on Wheels (projectmeal.org), your local United Way (in Google, search for "United Way" and your city or state, and look for volunteer opportunities that deal with feeding the hungry).

Start a club at school.

- Recruit a faculty sponsor so the club has credibility.

- Even if you opt to get involved with global efforts to feed hungry people, do something locally, too. For starters, call your county social services office, and check their Web site: That office knows where the hungry people are in your area and probably already has the channels to feed them. But they always need human help, and that's where your club enters the picture.

What can you do for ten minutes a day to help alleviate the hunger of one person in the world?

Into Your Heart, If Not Your Home

> Then he turned to his host. "When you put on a
> luncheon or a dinner," he said, "don't invite your
> friends, brothers, relatives, and rich neighbors.
> For they will repay you by inviting you back.
> Instead, invite the poor, the crippled, the lame,
> and the blind. Then at the resurrection of the
> godly, God will reward you for inviting those who
> could not repay you."
>
> Luke 14:12–14

> Jesus invited the poor and the outcasts to sit at
> his banquet table. Who are our dinner guests?
>
> Gerard Thomas Straub, in *When Did I See You Hungry?*

Inviting hungry people into your home is only one way to fulfill the spirit of what Jesus told his dinner host. How about starting with inviting them into your heart?

Take panhandlers, for instance. You're downtown, walking to the bus stop or to the theater, and a man you smell before you see catches your eye and asks for spare change for food. Right or wrong, you're not about to take him home ("Mom, I brought home, um, someone for dinner . . . "). There are issues galore here—your safety, not the least of them. Mental illness and addictions of all sorts are common among

140

the urban hungry, and you're simply not equipped to deal with such people.

Let's say that you decide to give the guy a buck, then keep walking. But how do you know he'll use the buck toward a burger, and not on another fifth of Old Crow?

It takes a little footwork, but if you're serious about feeding the hungry, one person at a time, this works:

- Find a Burger King or café or maybe even a restaurant who's owner shares your compassion for your city's hungry people. Just make sure the eatery is in the same area that the panhandlers are in.

- Create a meal-coupon system with the restaurant: That is, design and print coupons that you or anyone can buy for, say, five bucks each.

- Then, when you're approached on the street by panhandlers, you give them coupons instead of cash.

Some panhandlers, of course, will be ticked and just walk away because they really want cash to drink away. But those who want food will be grateful. And if you haven't exactly invited these men and women into your home, you've at least given them a peek into your heart.

Another way to follow the spirit of Jesus' words: When you're in a restaurant, be aware of people around you, and listen to your heart.

Case in point: A young migrant couple was driving through

San Francisco, headed to northern California where there
was an aunt they could stay with until they found jobs. They
saw a diner, parked, sat down at the counter, and opened a
menu. As their eyes skimmed the menu for the cheapest
meal, their faces showed serious anxiety, as did their voices as
they discussed it quietly among themselves. They hardly had
enough cash to buy a couple cups of chowder and have any
gas money left.

But it was good chowder, and it was a nice break from the
freeway. At the cash register near the door, the young man
pulled out his wallet.

"You owe us nothing," the cashier said. "That man over
there has already paid for you." She pointed to a middle-aged
man at the counter, hunched over a hamburger and coffee,
on the stool right next to theirs.

You can do this sort of thing. All it takes is open ears—and
an open heart.

Who's In Charge Here, Anyway?

> Happy are those who have the God of Israel as
> their helper, whose hope is in the LORD their God
> . . . who gives justice to the oppressed and food
> to the hungry.
>
> Psalm 146:5,7

God is the source of all good things, we are told. The creator of all. King of the world.

We also know that most of the good things we receive, we receive from other people. Food, shelter, clothing, transportation—human men and women are behind it. They manufactured the trusses for your house, trucked the jeans you ordered online to your doorstep, fabricated and welded the door panels for your '95 Honda.

But, you say, go back a step—it was God who created the trees from which came the lumber for the trusses . . . it was God who created the animal life eons ago that became petroleum to fuel the FedEx truck . . . it was God who made the earth's minerals that were refined into your Honda's steel parts.

Granted. This is true. But you've got to admit that, just as it is a mystery how Jesus could be God and man at the same time (a key Christian doctrine called the *Incarnation*),

143

it is also a mystery how things get done in this world. Is it God or is it us?

It's both. Somehow. It's a very fuzzy line between what God does and what we do. Even most miracles we read about in the Bible or that happen today occur through a human agent of some sort.

So what do we make of the ancient Jewish song whose lyrics say that God gives food to the hungry? Of course it was understood that God was the ultimate source of food. But God needs human hands to get that food to the hungry people who need it.

Just east of downtown San Diego, on Imperial Avenue, there is in a church yard a larger-than-life statue of a black Jesus. He stands there in his robe, his arms extended a little out in front of his body. But then you look closer and notice that, where you expect his hands to be, palm up in a typical Christ pose, there are no hands. Each arm ends in a stump at the wrist. And the sign on the pedestal of this statue reads, THE ONLY HANDS HE HAS ARE YOURS.

It is certainly God who feeds the hungry, but it is just as certain that you are needed in the chain of events required to feed hungry and chronically malnourished people.

The Mother of All Yard Sales

> Jesus told him, "If you want to be perfect, go and
> sell all you have and give the money to the poor,
> and you will have treasure in heaven. Then come,
> follow me."
>
> Matthew 19:21

"Sell all you have," Jesus said. He always did set the bar high. Not "some of your stuff," but "all you have."

We'll let the theologians debate about the fine points of how to interpret this verse. Meanwhile, the rest of us will face this truth: Radical discipleship (like selling everything you have and giving the money to the poor) is best practiced by Christians who are socially and financially independent. If you are part of a family or household, chances are you have domestic obligations that keep you from, say, selling everything you own.

But that's okay, because God doesn't measure the dollar value of a gift. God looks at your heart, at your motives, at the degree of sacrifice. For a Mercedes owner to give away her car may require less sacrifice than for you to give away your bicycle.

So let's believe that Jesus is delighted by whatever it is you can collect and sell for the benefit of hungry and poor people.

Where do you start? Her is how to go about setting up the
yard sale for selling all the stuff you prune.

- Plan how and when you'll sell the stuff you clean out.
  Recruit your friends to the fundraising effort, too, then
  pool all your stuff in one big yard sale—the bigger the
  sale, the more attractive it is to yard sale cruisers.

- Publicize the yard sale as widely as you can—through
  your church, your youth group, other churches, with
  posters or printed announcements on bulletin boards at
  Laundromats, cafés, grocery stores, etc.

- Also decide ahead of time: To what organization will
  you give your yard sale earnings? Or do you want to
  make a one-time donation to a national or international
  group? Ask your church for recommendations.

Whether this is a project you do alone, or whether you
enlist the help of your friends or youth group—follow Jesus'
words: Sell (some of) what you have and give it to the poor
and hungry. There's even a bonus for those that do this. (You
did read the last part of that verse above, didn't you?)

Have Another Helping . . .

Have Another Helping . . .

Y ou've read several Bible verses (if not chapters) in the past week or so. So consider this a Bible-reading Sabbath for yourself: You won't read any new Bible passages today, but you have a chance today to reflect, ruminate, consider, mull, and weigh what you've already read.

In fact, there's even space here to write down anything that's been boiling around in your head or your heart for the past few days. So if you're the writing type, write on.

THOUGHTS

What's making sense to you about all this hunger stuff so far?

What's not making sense?

FEELINGS

How does what you've read so far make you feel? Did anything in the Bible or in the readings stop you in your tracks, fry your brain, or otherwise rearrange how you feel about poverty, hunger, the hungry, and what the Bible says about them all?

QUESTIONS

What questions are still spinning in your head? What's still unclear to you? What questions do you wish you could ask *us*?

DECISION

Recall the previous ten or so readings in this book. (Yes, of course it's okay to flip back and review them now. . . . Finished? Good.) What one act or conversation or meeting can you realistically vow to do—or *start* doing—within the next ten days? The only criterion is that your act or conversation or meeting must in some way, if ever so small, begin to make at least one person or one family or one neighborhood less hungry.

Prune Your Possessions

Prune Your Possessions

Don't store up treasures here on earth, where they
can be eaten by moths and get rusty, and where
thieves break in and steal. Store your treasures
in heaven, where they will never become moth-eaten
or rusty and where they will be safe from thieves.

Matthew 6:19–20

Now that you've planned what you'll do with all your old stuff
you're gonna sell, it's time to collect it all. So first, get two
boxes: a SELL IT box for stuff you'll sell (for cash that you'll
donate to an organization that feeds the hungry) and a TOSS
IT box for stuff that's broken or hopelessly worn out. So
you'll be boxing some things and tossing others. Then . . .

- Adopt this rule of thumb and adhere to it ruthlessly: If
  you linger over a possession more than a couple seconds,
  box it or toss it. No second-guessing allowed. Tomorrow
  you'll be glad you removed it from your room.

- Start with your closet: If you haven't worn something
  there at least once this season, box it or toss it. Be ruth-
  less. Don't be distracted by thinking, "Well, this shirt is
  perfect if I ever climb Mt. Whitney." Face it—you'll
  never climb Mt. Whitney. If somehow you *do* end up

149

climbing Mt. Whitney and you need a shirt like that, then you can go buy one at a thrift store for two bucks.

- If some clothing needs minor mending and has needed it for a year, admit that you're really not gonna mend it, and make a quick decision whether to SELL it or TOSS it. In either case, it'll be out of your closet. (Doesn't living simpler feel better already?)

- Okay, so much for your closet—now for the rest of your room. That gift book from your aunt you've never read and have no intention of reading . . . a few of your stuffed animals that have no particularly sentimental significance . . . half-burned candles . . . posters that have been on your wall for three years now—prune your stuff with a vengeance. Sell it, all of it.

- If you really want to score with your parents, offer to do the same thing to the basement or garage. Maybe your mom or dad will even pitch in and help.

Clean it out, sell it, toss what you don't sell—and you'll be doing the hungry and yourself a favor.

Who in the World Is Hungry?

Rise during the night and cry out. Pour out your
hearts like water to the Lord. Lift up your hands
to him in prayer. Plead for your children as they
faint with hunger in the streets.

Lamentations 2:19

Here are some stats on hunger throughout the world, by the
numbers. Take a moment to pray for the people who are suffering around the world.

- More than 840 million people in the world are malnourished—799 million of them are from the developing world. More than 153 million of them are under the age of five.[1]

- Six million children under the age of five die every year as a result of hunger.[1]

- Of the 6.2 billion people in today's world, 1.2 billion live on less than $1 per day.[2]

- The proportion of South Asians living on less than $1 a day has fallen from 44 percent to 37 percent in the past ten years; of Africans, however, from 48 percent only to 47 percent.[3]

- The amount of money that the richest one percent of the world's people make each year equals what the poorest 57 percent make.[2]

- The richest 5 percent of the world's people have incomes 114 times that of the poorest 5 percent.[2]

- Malnutrition can severely affect a child's intellectual development. Children who have stunted growth due to malnutrition score significantly lower on math and language achievement tests than do well-nourished children.[4]

- Virtually every country in the world has the potential of growing sufficient food on a sustainable basis. The Food and Agriculture Organization of the United Nations has set the minimum requirement for caloric intake per person per day at 2,350. Worldwide, there are 2,805 calories available per person per day.[5]

- Fifty-four countries fall below that requirement—that is, they do not produce enough food to feed their populations, nor can they afford to import the necessary commodities to make up the gap. Most of these countries are in sub-Saharan Africa.[6]

- Each day in the developing world, more than thirty thousand children die from mostly preventable and treatable causes such as diarrhea, acute respiratory infections, measles, or malaria. These diseases are far more deadly to children who are stunted or underweight.[2]

- More than two million children each year have severe visual problems due to lack of vitamin A.[1]

- As in the U.S., preschool and school-age children around the world who experience severe hunger have higher levels of chronic illness, anxiety and depression, and behavior problems than children with no hunger, according to a recent study.[7]

SOURCES

1. State of Food Insecurity in the World 2002. Food and Agriculture Organization of the United Nations. *http://www.fao.org/docrep/005/y7352e/y7352e00.htm*

2. Human Development Report 2002, Deepening Democracy in a Fragmented World, United Nations Development Programme. *http://www.undp.org/hdr2002/*

3. "Secretary-General Warns World Falling Short of Millennium Summit Commitments," Press Release from UN Secretary-General Kofi Annan, October 1, 2002. *http://www.un.org/millenniumgoals/sg2079e.htm*

4. State of the World's Children 1998, UNICEF. *http://www.unicef.org/pubsgen/sowc98*

5. FAO database; numbers for the year 2000. *http://apps.fao.org/lim500/wrap.pl?FoodBalanceSheet&Domain=FoodBalanceSheet&Language=english*

6. Mapping of the Food Supply Gap 1998. Food and Agriculture Organization of the United Nations. *http://www.fao.org/*

7. Pediatrics, Vol. 110 No. 4, October 2002. *http://www.pediatrics.org/cgi/content/abstract/110/4/e41*

Americans Are Hungry, Too

Americans Are Hungry, Too

> My servants have never let others go hungry. I
> have never turned away a stranger but have opened
> my doors to everyone. Have I tried to hide my sins
> as people normally do, hiding my guilt in a closet?
>
> Job 31:31–33

Is hunger really a problem in the United States? When we think about hunger, we usually think in terms of mass starvation on other continents. But hunger is right here in our own backyard. Even in recent and more prosperous times, millions of U.S. citizens (including children) did not have access to enough food for an active, healthy life and were often forced to choose between relying on emergency food sources or going hungry.

The recent economic downturn has further complicated the efforts of millions of poor people to simply get by. In the autumn of 2002, the unemployment rate jumped in one month from 4.9 percent to 5.4 percent—the largest one-month jump in two decades. By early 2003 it had climbed to 5.8 percent and peaked in June at 6.4 percent.

Bottom line: In June 2003 there were 1,245,000 more people unemployed than eight months earlier. For families already struggling to make ends meet, losing a job can be catastrophic.[1]

Hunger in the U.S., by the numbers:

- Three percent of U.S. households experience hunger. That's nine million people, which includes three million children.[2]

- Thirty-four million people—including twelve million children—live in households where people have to skip meals or eat less to make ends meet. That means one in ten households are living with hunger or are at risk of hunger.[2]

- Preschool and school-aged children who experience severe hunger have higher levels of chronic illness, anxiety, depression, and behavior problems than children with no hunger, according to a recent study.[3]

- People facing hunger are increasingly turning to the food stamp program for assistance in feeding their families. Following years of decline, participation in the program has been on the rise over the past two years. In August 2002 (the last month for which data are available), 19.7 million people participated in the food stamp program. March 2002 was the first month since July 1998 in which the number of food stamp participants exceeded nineteen million.[4]

- Churches and charities are straining to serve rising requests for food from their pantries and soup kitchens, especially from working people.

- America's Second Harvest, the nation's largest network of food banks, reports that more than twenty-three million people turned to the agencies they serve in 2001—an increase of more than two million since 1997. Forty percent were from working families.[5]

Spend some time in prayer today to figure out exactly what you're going to do to make a difference in a world that's hurting.

SOURCES:
1. This material adapted from the FAQ Web page of Bread for the World.
   http://www.bread.org/hungerbasics/faq.html

2. Household Food Security in the United States, 2001. ERS Food Assistance and Nutrition Research Report No. FANRR-29, United States Department of Agriculture, October 2002.
   http://www.ers.usda.gov/publications/fanrr29/

3. *Pediatrics*, Vol. 110 No. 4, October 2002.
   http://www.pediatrics.org/cgi/content/abstract/110/4/e41

4. Food Stamp Caseloads are Rising, Joseph Llobrera, Center on Budget and Policy Priorities, November, 19, 2002.
   http://www.cbpp.org/1-15-02fa.htm

5. Hunger in America 2001, America's Second Harvest.
   http://www.secondharvest.org/whoshungry/hunger_stud y_intro.html

Have Fun, Sweat a Little— and Make Some Money in the Process

> Though they have been going through much trouble and hard times, their wonderful joy and deep poverty have overflowed in rich generosity. For I can testify that they gave not only what they could afford but far more. And they did it of their own free will.
>
> 2 Corinthians 8:2–3

So you've cleaned out your room and had a yard sale, or your room is perpetually tidy and needs no cleaning, or your room would take a week and a backhoe to clean and you don't have time for that right now.

So what are your fundraising options if you want to earn some money for a donation to the world's hungry? (Just about every idea here depends on good planning and publicity. So if you're inexperienced in this aspect, get help from a friend or adult who *is* experienced.)

30 Hour Famine. Join your youth group for this annual February fundraising event sponsored by World Vision. Ask your youth director about it and check out the 30 Hour Famine Web site (30hourfamine.org).

Costume party. Halloween or anytime is good for this. Give it an international theme. Charge admission. Award goofy prizes for Best Costume, Worst Costume, the Most Obviously Last-Minute Costume, Best Abstract Costume, Quirkiest Costume, Most Creative Interpretation of a Traditional Costume, etc.

Read-a-thon, walk-a-thon, bike-a-thon, skate-a-thon, whatever-a-thon. Collect pledges from family, friends and community members for each hour or mile students walk, bike, etc., or for each book read.

Are you artsy? Recruit your artistic friends to join you in creating works of art (or of craft) that you'll auction—proceeds, of course, to be donated to feeding the hungry. Up the ante by asking some real live local artists to donate a couple of their pieces, too.

Poetry reading. Ask your local independent or chain bookstore, or a café owner who is sympathetic to your cause, if you can hold a poetry reading on their premises. Sign up your friends and youth group members to read their own or other's poems related to poverty and hunger. Either charge admission or pass the hat halfway through the readings. Be sure to explain where the money will go. Call your local radio and TV stations and let them know what you're doing—it's free advertising for both you and the bookstore or café owner.

Community auction. Ask families, friends, and community businesses to donate skills, services, products, etc., to be auctioned off. Be creative: Just about *anyone* can auction themselves for a day of babysitting or museum-hopping with a small child. Teachers have been known to make videos in their classrooms over the course of the year then auction them off to parents. Restaurant and theater owners can donate dinners and seats to shows. This takes some serious organizing, but such an event can raise lots of money for your cause and will alert the community and get everyone involved as well.

And don't forget the ever-popular youth group fundraising options like bake sales (feature foods from the country you're donating money to), car washes, yard work, dog walking, etc.

Convert your awareness of world hunger and your compassion for the hungry into action! You can do it!

Why More Females
Than Males Are Hungry

Why More Females
Than Males Are Hungry

> Evil people steal land by moving the boundary
> markers. They steal flocks of sheep, and they even
> take donkeys from the poor and fatherless. A poor
> widow must surrender her valuable ox as collateral
> for a loan.
>
> Job 24:2–3

Seventy percent of the world's poor are female, UNICEF tells us. Poor people typically don't have enough to eat, or enough *nutritious* food to eat that will keep them healthy. So you could reasonably conclude that 70 percent of the world's *hungry* are female, too.

If you have feminist leanings, we can hear you say, "Aha! I just *knew* there was a gender slant to this world-hunger stuff. Once again, women take the brunt of the suffering."

You may have a point. Look at what happens far too often in our own North America: A guy and a girl with typically little education (i.e., they dropped out of high school, or at least stopped their schooling when they graduated from high school) get together and within five years have a couple of kids. With just a high-school diploma (if that), job options tend to be the minimum-wage sort. If the guy *does* land a ten-bucks-an-hour job—roofer, truck driver, mechanic, etc.—he's among the first to be laid off when the economy dips. So this family is always living on the edge, paycheck to paycheck, a family for whom a movie is a twice-a-year treat. They can't afford healthy food, so they buy inexpensive food—lots of processed foods like white bread and macaroni. A lot of their packaged and canned food is laced with sugar and MSG and nitrates. Fresh veggies are a rarity in their diet.

So the children's health is already on the line, though it's not particularly apparent. They certainly aren't underweight, which is the image you have of malnourished children.

Now say the father bails out—just up and leaves. A common situation. A family of two children have now lost their breadwinner, and if they were on the economic fringe before, they slip quickly into poverty now. The children's father starts over by himself or with another woman, while the children's mother applies for food stamps through AFDC (Aid for Families with Dependent Children, which fewer and fewer poor people are able to qualify for due to recent federal regulations).

You can safely assume that the father, freed of having to support a family of four, is able to now support just himself at least a little above the poverty level. So that's one *less* male in poverty and at least one *more* female in poverty—and probably more, if either or both of those kids are female.

Next time we'll explore what this tragic econo-gender scenario means for you.

If a Woman's in Crisis, She's
Probably Hungry, Too

If a Woman's in Crisis, She's Probably Hungry, Too

> Destruction is certain for the unjust judges, for those who issue unfair laws. They deprive the poor, the widows, and the orphans of justice. Yes, they rob widows and fatherless children!
>
> Isaiah 10:1–2

Let's assume you've already read Gender Economics 101 and understand how it is that more females than males on this planet are hungry. Globally and historically, men tend to be poor because of a disability of some sort. Women and children (most of whom are female), on the other hand, tend to be poor because these dependents have for some reason lost the household wage earner.

So what does this mean to you?

As usual, let's start close to home. Go to the women's resource center at a nearby university or junior college and you'll find that poverty and hunger are among the issues that the center's staffers have to address.

Go to any obstetrics or pediatrics clinic in your city and you'll find doctors and nurses fighting an uphill battle trying to keep poor pregnant women and poor mothers of newborns healthy—that is, eating enough and eating well.

Go to any women's crisis center or YWCA and you'll find poor and hungry people there.

We're not saying that males don't suffer or aren't hungry. It's just that, for whatever reason, females tend to bear the statistical brunt of poverty and the resulting hunger.

Where do you come in?

Here's where: Look for those agencies and offices and resource centers in your town that offer help to women and you'll find poor and hungry women. Their poverty and hunger is almost always part of the reason they need help. And you can make a dent in world hunger by helping these women's centers.

Does your church or denomination have a ministry to women? Not a Bible study or prayer ministry (although these are important), but ministries that care for the *bodies* of women and their children? If so, consider focusing your volunteer and fundraising efforts here.

If your church or denomination *doesn't* have such a program, get on-line and Google a search for "women's resource center" and your state or county or city. Click beyond all the reproductive health and domestic abuse issues you'll find—important stuff, but one thing at a time: Get your town's poor women eating well, and a lot of the other problems begin gradually clearing up, too.

A high schooler *can* make a difference in global hunger—and sometimes it's in starting close to home, one poor and malnourished mother at a time.

How Politics
and Economics Cause Hunger

How Politics and Economics Cause Hunger

> We growl like hungry bears; we moan like mournful
> doves. We look for justice, but it is nowhere to
> be found. We look to be rescued, but it is far
> away from us.
>
> Isaiah 59:11

Allow us to introduce you to three big, fat common causes of
an inadequate supply of opportunities and skills: political
causes, economic causes, and social causes.

POLITICAL CAUSES OF HUNGER

- *War* disrupts economic and social activity, not to mention creating refugees (those who must flee their
  homes if not their countries). War is a huge cause of
  hunger in developing nations.

- *Repression* usually affects specific social or ethnic
  groups. It denies full access to economic opportunities
  and political participation.

- *Public spending priorities* are often slanted toward mil-
  itary spending or security forces and away from public

investment—like education, health, and infrastructure (electricity, water, bus lines, and phone service, for example). Developing nations typically cannot afford both.

- *Corruption* is a fast track to hunger. Leaders greedy for power or wealth (those are usually synonymous) squander their nations' resources to enrich themselves and their associates. What this looks like: presidential palaces equipped with the ultimate in comfort and technology, luxury homes and penthouses for high-level government ministers—and in the streets joblessness, homelessness, poverty, and hunger.

ECONOMIC CAUSES OF HUNGER

In a word, *unemployment*. Simply not enough jobs. Three kinds of unemployment:

- *Frictional* unemployment is people between jobs. This is short-term—the frictionally unemployed usually pick up another job soon enough, so no one in the family goes hungry.

- *Cyclical* unemployment is what happens when a nation's or region's economy tanks. It's just part of the inevitable business cycle: A depressed economy is bound to come around, just as it will eventually improve again. Public-support programs are usually needed to keep the families of cyclically unemployed workers afloat, paying their bills, eating healthily.

- *Structural* unemployment puts people out of work for good, at least in a given industry. When assembly lines automate, for example, that spells the end of assembly-line workers, who will need to be retrained or educated for another job and financially supported during that transition.

THE END OF CLASS QUIZ (You have five minutes, after which we will grade these in class.)

1. What news have you heard recently about the lethal combination of war, repression, corruption, and hunger? In what nation or in what world region was the news occurring?

2. Have you experienced any of the three kinds of unemployment in your household? If so, how serious was it? Did you receive public assistance (like food stamps)? Or private assistance (like food from your church's Emergency Food Pantry)?

This material is adapted from "Mini-Course on Hunger" on the Web site of Oregon Bread for the World (*http://home.teleport.com/~breador/*).

Voluntary Hunger

> We fasted and earnestly prayed that our God would
> take care of us, and he heard our prayer.
>
> Ezra 8:23

Fasting—the deliberate, voluntary act of not eating for a specific reason, for a specific duration.

People fast today for all sorts of reasons. High school and college wrestlers fast in order to make weight on the day of a match. If you're scheduled to see your doctor for a physical exam and blood test, you'll probably be asked to fast for twelve hours prior to your appointment. If you're really serious about living a healthy lifestyle, claim some, you will fast one day a week just to clean out your system regularly. Political prisoners fast—sometimes to death—to protest their unjust imprisonment. Meanwhile, outside the prison walls, some sympathizers may fast in solidarity with the prisoner.

And don't forget the 30 Hour Famine, an annual February fasting and fundraising event sponsored by World Vision and participated in by thousands of youth groups around the country. During those thirty hours teenagers forgo meals, instead keeping themselves busy with service projects for the poor and hungry, with Bible studies, with meditation. If you join a youth group for the 30 Hour Famine, the only thing you'll taste is water and the barest something of what it's like to be hungry. (The money raised goes toward feeding the world's hungry.)

People in other cultures and at other times fasted for very different reasons. During grieving and mourning, for instance. Usually in our culture, after a funeral friends and family retire to a home and eat a meal. Not in ancient times. You grieved by *not* eating, by fasting.

When King Saul of ancient Israel and his royal sons were killed in battle, his enemies mutilated their bodies and hung them on the city wall for the buzzards to pick at. (Read about it in 1 Samuel 31: 11–13.) Aghast, Saul's surviving soldiers stole the bodies off the wall during the night, burned them, buried the remaining ash and bone bits—and fasted for seven days.

Or take Ezra, the scribe who oversaw the return of thousands of Jewish exiles in Persia back to Israel. "We fasted and earnestly prayed that our God would take care of us, and he heard our prayer," Ezra wrote (8:23). His reason for fasting was to add intensity to his prayer request—which is why King David fasted, too, when his infant son became critically ill. "I fasted and wept while the child was alive," said King David of Israel, "for I said, 'Perhaps the Lord will be gracious to me and let the child live.'" As it turned out, the child did not live, so David stopped mourning and picked up his fork and knife again.

To paraphrase what Solomon wrote (probably) and the Byrds made famous: There's a time for eating and a time to refrain from eating. For those who are well fed and healthy, it's a good thing to go hungry now and then.

How Fasting Goes Bad

For forty days and forty nights [Jesus] ate nothing and became very hungry.

Matthew 4:2

Over the course of human history, there have been all sorts of reasons to fast—among them, ceremonial fasting, such as God commanded the Jews in his law:

On the appointed day in early autumn, you must spend the day fasting and not do any work. This is a permanent law for you, and it applies to those who are Israelites by birth, as well as to the foreigners living among you. . . . It will be a Sabbath day of total rest, and you will spend the day in fasting. (Leviticus 16: 29, 31)

Makes you wonder where Christians got their idea of big holiday dinners. At any rate, you can see here that among all the private reasons to fast—while waiting on God for an answer to prayer, for example, or while grieving the death of a loved one—there were some public and national reasons to fast, too.

The only problem was that, like any public expression of private devotion, if you're not careful the public expression

169

gradually becomes the important thing to you, while the private devotion dries up. Which is exactly how the Pharisees earned their reputation during Jesus' time on earth. There is much historical evidence that that Jewish sect began as true lovers of God who wanted to obey Yahweh more than anything in the world. And by George, they got pretty good at it—so good, in fact, that Pharisees started paying more attention to what obedience *looked* like (impressive public prayers, studious avoidance of supposedly sinful places and people, etc.) than what obedience actually was: a humble heart, for starters.

The fasting God required as an expression of a humble and contrite heart soon became all show ("I fasted three days" . . . "Well, *I* fasted *five* days" . . . "That's nothing: *I* fasted so long that people gasped when I walked into synagogue on the Sabbath, I looked so weak and gaunt" . . .) and no heart. No humility. Which is why Jesus warned his disciples that when you fast, don't make it obvious, as the hypocrites do, who try to look pale and disheveled so people will admire them for their fasting. I assure you, that is the only reward they will ever get. But when you fast, comb your hair and wash your face. Then no one will suspect you are fasting except your Father, who knows what you do in secret. And your Father, who knows all secrets, will reward you.

So yes, there's a time for ceremonial fasting. (When's the last time your pastor asked the congregation to fast in order to seek God's mind in a decision?) But first things first: Don't let your public expression of humility—whether it's fasting as a group, praying publicly, or sharing the gospel with a friend—run ahead of your actual, inner humility.

And Now, a Word about Something Other Than Food

> God blesses those who are hungry and thirsty for
> justice, for they will receive it in full.
>
> Matthew 5:6

Let's get our minds off our stomachs for a minute and think about other kind of hungers.

Still, we're half animal, so it's forgivable if when we hear words like *hunger* or *food*, we think of our stomachs and start smelling fried chicken or cherry cheesecake. Even Jesus' disciples didn't get it. Once Jesus remarked offhandedly that his disciples would do well to beware the yeast of the religious leaders. And the disciples said, "DOH! Bread—we forgot to bring bread with us. That's what you mean, right, Lord?"

"How could you even think I was talking about *food?*" replied an exasperated Jesus, who then explained, probably slowly and in small words, that he was referring not to literal yeast but to false teaching, which infected everything just like yeast spreads throughout dough (Matthew 16: 5–12).

The disciples apparently didn't learn the lesson (are we surprised?). Another time the disciples urged Jesus to slow down from all his preaching and teaching and eat a bite. "No," he said. "I have food you don't know about" (John 4: 31–32).

171

He was plain as day, however, when, quoting the Torah, he said that "people need more than bread for their life; they must feed on every word of God" (Matthew 4: 4).

To this day you will hear teachers, preachers, and speakers refer to a new Christian's early doctrinal diet as "milk"— easily digestible food for the beginnings of spiritual growth. Solid food would come later, Paul pointed out (1 Cor. 3:1–2).

Whoever wrote the letter to the Hebrew Christians (theologians are divided on who was the author of this unsigned letter) pushed the image further—and boy, was she a tad frustrated, or what?

> You have been Christians a long time now, and you ought to be teaching others. Instead, you need someone to teach you again the basic things a beginner must learn about the Scriptures. You are like babies who drink only milk and cannot eat solid food. And a person who is living on milk isn't very far along in the Christian life and doesn't know much about doing what is right. Solid food is for those who are mature, who have trained themselves to recognize the difference between right and wrong and then do what is right. (Hebrews 5:12–14)

What is food to you? That is, what energizes and satisfies you?

Have Another Helping . . .

Have Another Helping . . .

Y ou've read several Bible verses (if not chapters) in the past week or so. So consider this a Bible-reading Sabbath for yourself: You won't read any new Bible passages today, but you have a chance today to reflect, ruminate, consider, mull, and weigh what you've already read.

In fact, there's even space here to write down anything that's been boiling around in your head or your heart for the past few days. So if you're the writing type, write on.

THOUGHTS

What's making sense to you about all this hunger stuff so far?

What's not making sense?

FEELINGS

How does what you've read so far make you feel? Did anything in the Bible or in the readings stop you in your tracks, fry your brain, or otherwise rearrange how you feel about poverty, hunger, the hungry, and what the Bible says about them all?

QUESTIONS

What questions are still spinning in your head? What's still unclear to you? What questions do you wish you could ask *us*?

DECISION

Recall the previous ten or so readings in this book. (Yes, of course it's okay to flip back and review them now. . . . Finished? Good.) What one act or conversation or meeting can you realistically vow to do—or *start* doing—within the next ten days? The only criterion is that your act or conversation or meeting must in some way, if ever so small, begin to make at least one person or one family or one neighborhood less hungry.

What Hunger Drives One To

When he finally came to his senses, he said to himself, "At home even the hired men have food enough to spare, and here I am, dying of hunger!"

Luke 15:17

Hunger is a killer and a destroyer—not only of physical lives but of dreams, of energy, of families.

For those of us who typically get enough to eat—whose health isn't compromised by always being so tight on money that all we can afford is filling food instead of nutritious food—for us occasional, self-imposed hunger can be a good thing. Like fasting, for instance.

Even if it isn't always self-imposed, hunger can do good things in us. As in Jesus' story of the Prodigal Son, who squandered his inheritance in record time and ended up dead broke in a job that didn't exactly have a future: hog slopping. His dumbness finally broke through to him when he realized that the hogs had it better than he did: at least they had a sty to call their own and regular and plentiful meals.

It was hunger—literal, stomach-panged hunger—that brought the young man to his senses and turned him toward home and a father who loved him.

Again, a hunger that threatened to become starvation

175

prodded Jacob's family toward physical salvation (and a family reunion).

Not that God *causes* hunger and famine and starvation—then or now—in order to do some good work. To claim that God *causes* hunger and all the economic, psychological, domestic, and financial catastrophes that follow from hunger would be to make God into a horrific deity who concocted pain and suffering for some humans in order to do good to others.

People, Satan, whoever create the evil, the suffering, the pain (explain some theologians)—and God somehow *turns it to good*. God didn't cause the Holocaust, the Black Plague, the Srebrenica massacre (of seven thousand Muslim men and boys by Bosnian Serb soldiers in 1995—the worst massacre in Europe since World War II). God doesn't cause these nightmarish horrors—yet at the same time, there is no evil, no tragedy, no person that is beyond God's power to redeem. What in your experience, in your life, in the life of a friend, at school, at work, in youth group—what went horribly awry, but in hindsight you see that God redeemed for good? What is going horribly awry for you (or for someone you know) *now?* Is it impossible or easy—or somewhere in between—to have faith that God can indeed redeem even this for good?

Hard Questions for Bible Believers

> Then this message came to Zechariah from the
> LORD: "This is what the LORD Almighty says:
> Judge fairly and honestly, and show mercy and
> kindness to one another. Do not oppress widows,
> orphans, foreigners, and poor people. And do not
> make evil plans to harm each other."
>
> Zechariah 7:8–10

First hard question: are these words from the Lord through the Jewish prophet Zechariah intended as divine commands for today as well as for Zech's day? If so, exactly who ought to be heeding them? Churches? National governments? Local governments? Families? Individuals?

All sorts of hard questions lurk here, where the words of an ancient prophet intersect with our twenty-first-century techno-lives. Yet if we claim to be biblical Christians, we need to face issues that Zechariah raises. Questions like these:

- Why did the U.S. defend the global patent rights of highly profitable pharmaceutical companies for so long, knowing this would keep AIDS drugs unaffordable to poor African countries?

- Philip Yancey, Christian columnist, points out that during the 1979–89 war with the Soviet Union, Afghans lost a third of their dwelling places. Yet thanks to their tradition of hospitality, not a single person went homeless. Why does the richest nation in the world (that would be the U.S.) have so many homeless people, while one of the poorest nations has none?

- How do we explain that, as of four years ago, of the world's twenty-nine developed nations, the U.S. had the second-highest child poverty rate, exceeded only by Mexico?

These are hard questions. So hard, some say, that there are no easy answers. Others say the answers are as clear as the sun over Tucson, except that our current political and economic systems would have to be overhauled to let those clear answers work.

Chances are, you're not going to overhaul the system while you're in high school (though you might have a hand in it later). Right now, however, you can overhaul your attitude toward the poor in your town, your nation, your world. You might even be able to overhaul the poverty of *one person*, somewhere, from despair to hope.

Social Causes of Hunger

Social Causes of Hunger

> You fat sheep push and butt and crowd my sick and
> hungry flock until they are scattered to distant
> lands.
>
> Ezekiel 34:21

In the previous session of our mini-course on hunger we explored two big fat causes of hunger: political and economic causes. Here's the third one—*social* causes of hunger—of which there are three: *family stresses*, *under-education*, and *unethical discrimination*.

Family stresses

You just can't overestimate families as primary social institutions. By all measures, families are *the* factor when it comes to creating a child's self-image, setting expectations for education and jobs, and opening them up to a wide world that needs their contributions. When families screw up here, children can grow up in an environment of despair and hopelessness—which, more often than not, leads directly or indirectly into poverty.

- *Economic stresses* can draw families together, but more often they damage them. Real wages—that is, what it costs to live against what you're paid—have been declining for the past twenty years, so that even having a steady job isn't enough to get a family out of poverty:

- A full-time minimum-wage job provides around $12,000 a year—not even near enough to raise a family of four out of poverty.

- Two-thirds of poor families have at least one working member—though it's usually part-time or seasonal work.

- *Health care stresses* occur when workers have no health insurance—which means, of course, that their children aren't covered, either.

- *Child care* is a vital need for working parents, but it's beyond the reach of many poor families.

- *Single parent families* are just plain difficult for a mom or dad to balance—for it's usually a juggling act between earning income and rearing children. Children raised in single-parent households are more likely to be poor—and remain poor when they grow up. Child-support enforcement, child care, and health care are vital needs for these families.

Undereducation

If families are our top social institution, then our educational system is number two. Today's jobs increasingly rely on higher levels of education. Being without such education hurts a person's income-earning potential, and consequently puts her at risk of hunger.

Unethical discrimination

Equal opportunity—the opposite of discrimination—is a basic principle of our society. It should characterize how we go about business—from our educational system to our market economies. The most efficient outcomes can be achieved only if everyone gets the chance to develop their potential. Of course there will always be inequality of result—some people work harder, smarter, or get better breaks—but really now, unethical opportunities that are arbitrarily given to some favored ones and withheld from others should be eliminated.

THE END OF CLASS QUIZ (No, you may not go to the lavatory during this quiz.)

1. When was the last time your family was broke? Or if not flat broke, was financially squeezed enough to make everyone nervous or irritable? Did you emerge from the crisis? How?

2. Do you live in a single-parent home? If your family went from two parents to one parent recently, what stresses, if any, do you experience now that you didn't before?

This material is adapted from "Mini-Course on Hunger" on the Web site of Oregon Bread for the World (*http://home.teleport.com/~breador/*).

Have Another Helping . . .

Have Another Helping . . .

You've read several Bible verses (if not chapters) in the past week or so. So consider this a Bible-reading Sabbath for yourself: You won't read any new Bible passages today, but you have a chance today to reflect, ruminate, consider, mull, and weigh what you've already read.

In fact, there's even space here to write down anything that's been boiling around in your head or your heart for the past few days. So if you're the writing type, write on.

THOUGHTS

What's making sense to you about all this hunger stuff so far?

What's not making sense?

FEELINGS

How does what you've read so far make you feel? Did anything in the Bible or in the readings stop you in your tracks, fry your brain, or otherwise rearrange how you feel about poverty, hunger, the hungry, and what the Bible says about them all?

QUESTIONS

What questions are still spinning in your head? What's still unclear to you? What questions do you wish you could ask *us*?

DECISION

Recall the previous ten or so readings in this book. (Yes, of course it's okay to flip back and review them now. . . . Finished? Good.) What one act or conversation or meeting can you realistically vow to do—or *start* doing—within the next ten days? The only criterion is that your act or conversation or meeting must in some way, if ever so small, begin to make at least one person or one family or one neighborhood less hungry.

But It's So . . . *Secular*

So Paul, standing before the Council, addressed
them as follows: "Men of Athens, I notice that you
are very religious, for as I was walking along I
saw your many altars. And one of them had this
inscription on it—'To an Unknown God.' You have
been worshiping him without knowing who he is, and
now I wish to tell you about him."

Acts 17:22–23

Today's reading isn't for everyone—just for those of you who,
when you read or hear or talk about world hunger, you get this
vague but persistent feeling that you're playing on the world's
turf here (it sounds so *secular* and all). Doesn't even world
hunger take a distant back seat to the eternally more significant concerns of salvation, righteousness, and eternal life?

When St. Paul arrived in Athens and observed the poly-
theism of the place, he quickly signed up for a time slot on
Mars Hill, where the city's brainiacs met to debate the latest
philosophies circulating around the Mediterranean world. Of
late, they had heard rumors of a Jewish sect, whose mar-
tyred messiah was said to have risen from the dead. Needless
to say, they became *very* interested when Paul opened his
mouth and not only confessed to being a follower of this cult,

but asserted that the God of his "cult" was the same deity who was honored by Athens's altar to the Unknown God.

So what might the apostle say today, if he happened to arrive in Rome on an Alitalia red-eye and catch a cab to the offices of the Food and Agriculture Organization of the United Nations there on Viale delle Terme di Caracalla?

Paul exits the cab, pays the driver (tipping him generously), and strides into the reception hall, where he sees Rwandans and Russians, Guatemalans and Burmese mingling around sautéed shrimp and Chardonnay. He looks for the lectern, walks to it, and clears his throat in the microphone. The delegates look up then glance at their programs to confirm who this little man is that they can barely see over the top of the lectern.

So what would St. Paul say? We'll never know, since he did his work, wrote his letters, preached his sermons, and served his jail terms in the first, not the twenty-first century. But if Acts 17 is any clue, you can bet that he would start by establishing that behind the FAO's passion to eradicate world hunger forever is the heart of Jehovah God and his Son Jesus Christ—that, in fact, in the delegates' desire to rid the world of the suffering of hunger, they are right on the same page with the Creator of the universe.

Now *that* would get their attention.

Don't Hold Your Breath

Don't Hold Your Breath

> It was by faith that Sarah together with Abraham
> was able to have a child, even though they were too
> old and Sarah was barren. Abraham believed that God
> would keep his promise. And so a whole nation came
> from this one man, Abraham, who was too old to have
> any children—a nation with so many people that,
> like the stars of the sky and the sand on the
> seashore, there is no way to count them.
>
> Hebrews 11:11–12

A problem as huge as hunger—not necessarily global hunger, just hunger in your own city—well, you just can't get your mind around it, it's so big and layered and complicated.

It will take time—probably a long time—of sacrificial and coordinated effort to make sure that the world's hungry and malnourished people get enough to eat.

But just because things may not improve measurably in your lifetime is no reason to throw in the towel and not do *anything*.

Take Woodrow Wilson, the U.S. president who literally worked himself to death trying in vain to convince Congress to join the League of Nations, which Wilson had helped create, and which virtually all of Western Europe joined, along with some other world powers. Granted, the League didn't do what it was intended to do—prevent another world war. But toward the end of World War II, twenty-one years after the death of Wilson, U.S. president Franklin Delanor Roosevelt said enough was enough and that *nobody* wanted another of these wars, thank you. By that time Congress saw the light, too, and the League of Nations got a makeover and a new name, and—*voila!*—the United Nations was born: an organization that, say what you will about its efficiency, has devoted its sixty years of existence to restoring peace to warring regions, jobs and stability to impoverished families, and food to starving people.

"The difficult we do immediately," the saying goes, "the impossible takes a little longer." Longer than your lifetime, maybe—but making a dent in world hunger *can* happen.

Prayer Lists for a Lifetime

> Keep on praying.
>
> 1 Thessalonians 5:17

You want a prayer list? Start here, and check back every month for updates:

> Go to the Global Information and Early Warning System on Food and Agriculture (GIEWS) at ***www.fao.org/giews/english/giewse.htm*** and click on the "Food Outlook" for the current month.

Here, for example, is a summary of some of the September 2003 outlook—and there's plenty of situations and millions of people to pray for here. In fact, divide up the continents or countries among your youth group and pray on!

As of early September 2003, some thirty-eight countries face serious food shortages requiring international food assistance.

Eastern Africa

- *Sudan:* Recent heavy rains and floods in parts have killed a number of people, displaced thousands, destroyed or damaged crops, and increased the likelihood of serious localized food shortages.

188

- *Eritrea:* Serious and widespread food shortages persist due to last year's drought, poverty, and the lingering effects of the war with Ethiopia. About 2.3 million people are now reported to be facing severe food shortages. Of these, about 1.4 million are reported to be drought affected.

- *Tanzania:* Prolonged drought conditions in several parts have affected a large number of households with an estimated 1.9 million people in need of food assistance.

- *Uganda:* The humanitarian situation in northern and eastern parts has worsened due to escalation of conflict. Recent fighting between Government forces and rebels has displaced more than 820,000 people, bringing the total number in need of emergency assistance to more than 1.6 million.

Southern Africa

- *Zimbabwe:* 5.5 million people, or half of the country's population, are in need of emergency food aid as a result of drought and the prevailing economic problems.

- *Angola*: Despite the end of the civil war and a good cereal harvest this year, food aid is required for 1.4 million people, mainly returnees and vulnerable groups.

- *Malawi, Zambia, Swaziland, and Lesotho:* Emergency food assistance is also required in areas affected by localized crop failure and for those affected by HIV/AIDS.

Asia

- *China:* While central, eastern, and southern regions have suffered the worst floods since 1991, the southern region is also suffering from drought.

- *Indonesia:* has suffered from a severe drought this year, while a powerful typhoon hit vast agricultural areas in northern Luzon in the Philippines with an estimated loss of 446,000 tons of maize.

- *Bangladesh:* Some 45,000 people have been displaced by floods and many rice seedbeds have been destroyed.

- *Mongolia:* has suffered the worst flooding since 1982 after droughts in recent years.

- *North Korea:* The current crop prospects are favorable, but the country suffers from severe chronic food shortages.

Europe

Food assistance continues to be necessary for refugees, the internally displaced and vulnerable people in *Serbia* and *Montenegro*, and in *Chechnya* in the Russian Federation.

Poor Jesus

> Listen to me, dear brothers and sisters. Hasn't God chosen the poor in this world to be rich in faith? Aren't they the ones who will inherit the Kingdom he promised to those who love him?
>
> James 2:5–6

It can be so frustrating, being Christians in the wealthiest part of the world, to hear Bible verses like this. What's with this poverty-is-precious stuff? What does it mean? Even churches and Christian organizations are in the business of raising money, not spending it, aren't they?

Probably because culture sets the tone of religion. Always has, always will. Currently, it appears, culture is molding a kind of Christianity that permits upper-middle-class Americans to feel justified in their affluence as long as they share some of it now and then with the less affluent. Hey, that's fine. At least they're sharing it. But do such families get their feelings from their Bible or from their culture? Just a question.

The bottom line is that Christians of all times and places need to stay close to the heart of Jesus in discerning what it means for them to obey God, regardless of how their culture tells them to interpret the Bible.

But you've got to admit that it *is* interesting, isn't it, that of all the socioeconomic levels God could have chosen for his Son, Jesus, to grow up and live his adult life in, it was a poor one. Most theologians feel safe assuming this because, however successful a craftsman his carpenter father Joseph may have been, he apparently died early: There is no mention of him beyond Jesus' twelfth year (Luke 2). The next time we read about Jesus in the Gospels, he's thirty and doing his debut miracle at a friend's wedding—and Joseph is nowhere in sight. To all appearances, Mary is his only parent. Any doubt about Joseph's early death is removed when Jesus, dying on the cross, retains consciousness long enough to ask his disciple John to take care of his mother for him.

So why did God inject his Son, Jesus, into an economically marginal family that seemingly lost its breadwinner and probably sank into poverty? Why didn't God arrange the birth of Jesus into a priestly family? Or a merchant family?

Maybe because there's something deep in Christianity, in God's heart in fact, about poverty. Poverty throws you upon the mercy of God. It makes you trust more. It gives you first empathy and then compassion for others who are poor. Economic poverty is a constant reminder of our spiritual poverty, were it not for the grace of God.

Being economically comfortable, on the other hand, tends to separate us from a healthy dependence on God and from compassion for others. Don't ask us why this is. It just is.

Hunger Solutions

Hunger Solutions

> If you have two coats, give one to the poor. If
> you have food, share it with those who are hungry.
>
> Luke 3:11

The causes of hunger are many, and so are the solutions. Solving hunger, in fact, requires addressing both short-term and long-term needs.

Meeting the **short-term** needs of the poor means providing food, health care, shelter, and personal safety. Unless people have *these* basic needs met, they can't focus on the long-term solutions of education and self-development.

It's short-term needs that U.S. welfare programs have traditionally tried to meet. Temporary Assistance for Needy Families (TANF), food stamps, Medicaid—benefits like these are designed to meet families' short-term needs, but by no means lift families out of poverty. Benefits usually end as soon as a family makes any effort to improve their lot, which saves the government money in the short run, but adds greatly to long-term costs because the system discourages poor persons' efforts to improve themselves.

Meeting the **long-term needs** of the poor means giving them job opportunities and access to the training, education, and support services they need to take advantage of them.

Yet even if jobs and education are available, most poor people *still* can't take advantage of them without such support services as health care, child care, and transportation. (Are you beginning to see how many barriers there are to self-sufficiency if you're poor—even if you have the desire to escape poverty?)

About jobs: Steady, hard work ought to be the way to rise out of poverty. Yet it's not when child care, health care, and housing cost so much a family has to skimp on food.

The heart of the problem—and the solution—lies in these long-term areas of jobs (that pay enough to help workers rise above poverty) and education. Failing here as a nation only increases the cost of the short-term programs.

THE END OF CLASS QUIZ (You may quietly leave the room when you've finished.)

1. What are your feelings about food stamps? Ever use them? Ever know someone who did?
2. What do you feel is the responsibility of those who *don't* need public assistance toward those who *do*?

This material is adapted from "Mini-Course on Hunger" on the Web site of Oregon Bread for the World (*http://home.teleport.com/~breador/*).

Do You, Christian, Take Poverty to Be
Thy Lawfully Wedded Spouse?

Do You, Christian, Take Poverty to Be Thy Lawfully Wedded Spouse?

> You know how full of love and kindness our Lord
> Jesus Christ was. Though he was very rich, yet for
> your sakes he became poor, so that by his poverty
> he could make you rich.
>
> 2 Corinthians 8:9

If Jesus had an economically marginal childhood he was clearly
in poverty up to his ears when he left home and struck out on
his own. "Foxes have dens to live in, and birds have nests,"
Jesus once remarked, "but I, the Son of Man, have no home
of my own, not even a place to lay my head" (Luke 9: 58). He
was always accepting a dinner invitation here, a guest bedroom there. One thing you never read in the Gospels is, "And
after he healed the multitudes, Jesus went home."

One moment, he was as rich as God; the next, he was
born as a human in an animal stall, of all places. And all so we
could become rich.

Follow that?

Well, we don't either, exactly. Which only goes to show
why our faith is often such a mystery.

Medieval Christian priests and theologians read such verses
in the Bible—about Jesus being poor, about the poor having an

easier time attaining holiness than the rich—then looked around them at their own church and thought, *I, for one, will need to be poor if I'm ever going to be holy*. Church authorities quickly recognized a good thing when they saw it, and soon monasteries were springing up all over Europe.

Fundamental to being a monk were vows of poverty, chastity, and obedience. If you wanted to be a monk, then you vowed to be poor, to be celibate (no sex), and to live humbly in community with your brother monks instead of wanting to be in charge.

Not that riches, sex, and worldly authority and honor are sins. They're *hindrances*, the Bible teaches, innocent in themselves and not forbidden to Christians. In fact, Christians can be plenty holy and indulge in these three. But . . . well, when sin comes knocking, it's usually at one of these doors. So Christians from the Middle Ages to today who want to voluntarily free themselves of even these legitimate circumstances—these Christians become monks.

Even if you never become a monk, you've gotta admire the motive. Your only question is this: How will *you* reflect Christ's voluntary poverty for our sakes?

That's okay, take your time. It's a hard question. Takes some a lifetime to answer.

Hunger Isn't Just a Foreign Tragedy

Hunger Isn't Just a Foreign Tragedy

Jesus soon saw a great crowd of people climbing the hill, looking for him. Turning to Philip, he asked, "Philip, where can we buy bread to feed all these people?"

John 6:5

The hospital could be anywhere. On the desk of a medical worker is a stack of patient charts. The following are typical reports:

- Four-year-old with stunted growth, anemia, hair loss (a sure sign of malnutrition).

- Twenty-month-old failing to thrive; has one meal per day, usually soup.

- Mother and three children who upon admittance to hospital stuffed food into their mouths, having had nothing to eat for three days.

- Pregnant woman, gained one pound over seven months.

- Mother of four who decides each day which two of her kids get something to eat.

Furthermore, a third of the children that show up in this hospital's emergency room are underweight or stunted in growth; many of the infants have severe diarrhea and dehydration.

"What we see are clear, measurable health effects of hunger and malnutrition, proof that more and more families do not have enough money to buy food." So concludes Dr. Effie Ellis, pediatrician at Cook County Hospital.[1]

In Chicago.

You may not know them (then again, you may), but within ten miles of you in the good old U.S. of A., a lot of people are hungry. It's a single mom who has to choose whether the salary from her minimum-wage job will go to buy food or pay the rent. She's gotta have a roof over their heads, she figures, so she pays the rent and skimps on food. It's a classmate of yours—or a student in a nearby high school—who struggles to concentrate on her schoolwork because her family couldn't afford dinner the night before. (Not couldn't afford to eat out, but couldn't afford dinner, period.) It's an older couple who has worked hard their entire lives only to find their savings wiped out by unavoidable medical bills or their retirement by corporate theft.

It's not because adults aren't willing to work. There are lots of reasons why Americans are unable to feed their families. For starters, it's a fact (not a pretty one, either) that the U.S. has the highest wage inequality of any industrialized nation, because of the income gap between well-educated professionals and workers with limited education.[2] People can work full-time, low-skill jobs and still not make enough money to maintain a basic standard of living—buying food, paying their rent and medical bills, buying clothes for their children, and affording a car so that they can travel to work.

The troubling part is that providing just food seldom gets to the roots of hunger. Sure, food pantries in your church, in your city and county provide urgently needed help. But *food assistance* is less important to overcoming hunger than *job opportunities*. Remember, hunger is a result of poverty. Empowering people, providing them with opportunities, or helping them cultivate an awareness of what they can do to improve their lives—these are among the most important ways of overcoming hunger and poverty.

Maybe for you, the first step is making *yourself* aware of the world of hurt outside your door, your circle of friends, your dreams for your future. Think about opening your door or your circle of friends or even your dreams to people possibly unlike you. How could you not, if you call yourself a Christian?

1. From *Living Hungry in America* by J. Larry Brown and H. F. Pizer (Mentor, 1987).

2. From *Hunger in a Global Economy*, annual report on the state of world hunger (Bread for the World Institute, 1998).

Have Another Helping . . .

Have Another Helping . . .

Y ou've read several Bible verses (if not chapters) in the past week or so. So consider this a Bible-reading Sabbath for yourself: You won't read any new Bible passages today, but you have a chance today to reflect, ruminate, consider, mull, and weigh what you've already read.

In fact, there's even space here to write down anything that's been boiling around in your head or your heart for the past few days. So if you're the writing type, write on.

THOUGHTS

What's making sense to you about all this hunger stuff so far?

What's not making sense?

FEELINGS

How does what you've read so far make you feel? Did anything in the Bible or in the readings stop you in your tracks, fry your brain, or otherwise rearrange how you feel about poverty, hunger, the hungry, and what the Bible says about them all?

QUESTIONS

What questions are still spinning in your head? What's still unclear to you? What questions do you wish you could ask *us*?

DECISION

Recall the previous ten or so readings in this book. (Yes, of course it's okay to flip back and review them now. . . . Finished? Good.) What one act or conversation or meeting can you realistically vow to do—or *start* doing—within the next ten days? The only criterion is that your act or conversation or meeting must in some way, if ever so small, begin to make at least one person or one family or one neighborhood less hungry.

TRANSIT

Where Life Goes

www.transitbooks.com

In this completely rewritten student edition of *Search for Significance* Robert McGee will help you learn how to be free to enjoy Christ's love while no longer basing your self-worth on your accomplishments or the opinions of others. With practical application points, youth challenges, and journaling space, this version of the classic book is perfect for every teen.

0-8499-4446-5

Michael W. Smith has seen with clarity the spiritual poverty and emotional numbness of teens who are out of touch with God's love. *It's Time to Be Bold* is a call to commitment for all believers, a personal and heartfelt cry rallying youth to follow Christ's example. Drawing from events in his own life, Michael discusses with relevance the essential issues of living out extreme faith.

084994435X

Teens face challenges at school-struggling to make the right decisions when they are just starting to learn who they really are. In *The Rules*, you will understand God's perfect plan for your life using the basic boundaries that He has set for you. You will clearly see the benefits that will come when you follow God's rules for living the good life.

0849944171

Mission: Africa is the ultimate resource on missions for today's teens. After completing this study, any youth group or community will be fully prepared to take a trip to Africa or distribute medicine, train workers, or find homes for orphans from their own hometown. *Mission: Africa* provides the ultimate challenge for any teen who is passionate about foreign missions!

0849944260

Two Guys,
One Mission,
Zero Guarantees!

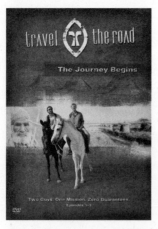

Travel the Road #1VHS (1-4003-0369-9)
Travel the Road#1 DVD (1-4003-0370-2)
Travel the Road #2 VHS (1-4003-0369-9)
Travel the Road #2 DVD (1-4003-0370-2)
Travel the Road #3 VHS (1-4003-0395-8)
Travel the Road #3 DVD (1-4003-0399-6)

Travel the world with extreme missionaries Tim Scott and Will Decker as they set out to take the gospel to the ends of the earth. Viewers will travel virtually through 25 countries and over 40,000 miles in this one-of-a-kind "reality TV" video/DVD series. Capturing the attention of a young audience-similar to MTV's The Real World or CBS's Survivor-Travel the Road mixes cutting-edge video production, graphics, and fast-paced story lines. In Episodes 1-3, you'll get a first-hand account of the danger and adventure of real-life mission work in remote areas of Burundi and India (including New Delhi, Bombay, Taj Mahal and the Ganges River). Fantastic for youth groups or small group viewing, Travel the Road is a great way to introduce young people to the realities and adventure of world missions.

FED UP?

YOU KNOW YOU ARE.

Fed up with people who think your generation is a lost cause. Fed up with those who believe you and your friends lack spiritual purpose . . . have misplaced your priorities . . . and are too afraid to stand out and make a difference. You're fed up with people who think you just don't care, don't want to and don't need to.

DO SOMETHING ABOUT IT.

Here's a great way for you and your friends to prove everyone wrong. It's a chance to transform your life more into the image of Christ's through a spiritually rewarding experience. After all, you'll be saving lives and showing everyone you really do care.

DO THE 30 HOUR FAMINE.

Make a statement. Have fun. And save the lives of hungry children around the world.

FREE VIDEO!

TAKE THIS TO YOUR YOUTH LEADER!
TELL YOUR YOUTH LEADER YOU WANT TO DO THE FAMINE.

Last weekend in February
(but you can do it any time)

Call 1.800.7.FAMINE NOW or visit www.30hourfamine.org to receive more <u>FREE</u>, no-obligation information.

World Vision

30 HOUR FAMINE

it's about saving kids' Lives

152165